Praise for

Connecting the Dots

"When God sends you on an adventure, He rarely gives all the details, but you can be sure He'll be with you on the journey, even if you can't see Him all the time. My friend Joël has written a book that's like an adventure map to help you keep your perspective lifted and see that God really is up to something amazing, even when life doesn't make sense."

—**Bob Goff,** honorary consul of Uganda and *New York Times* bestselling author of *Love Does*; *Everybody, Always*; *Dream Big*; *Live in Grace, Walk in Love*; and *Undistracted*

"I've been on many adventures with Joël—we've hiked the Inca Trail to Machu Picchu and rafted the Colorado River into the Grand Canyon. This book feels like one of those adventures. It will stretch your faith in tough times and help you find your way forward."

—**Mark Batterson,** pastor of National Community Church, Washington, D.C., and *New York Times* bestselling author of *The Circle Maker* and *Win the Day*

"God not only has a plan for your life; He also has a process to fulfill it. In *Connecting the Dots*, my friend Joël Malm provides a roadmap to help you gain perspective on how God works to prepare you for what He has planned for you!"

—**John Bevere,** bestselling author, minister, and cofounder of Messenger International and MessengerX

Connecting the Dots

Connecting the Dots

WHAT GOD IS DOING WHEN LIFE DOESN'T MAKE SENSE

Joël Malm

SALEM
BOOKS
an imprint of Regnery Publishing
Washington, D.C.

Cataloging-in-Publication data on file with the Library of Congress.

ISBN: 978-1-68451-329-1
eISBN: 978-1-68451-398-7

Library of Congress Control Number: 2022949159

Published in the United States by
Salem Books
An Imprint of Regnery Publishing
A Division of Salem Media Group
Washington, D.C.
www.SalemBooks.com

Manufactured in the United States of America

10 9 8 7 6 5 4 3 2 1

Books are available in quantity for promotional or premium use. For information on discounts and terms, please visit our website: www.SalemBooks.com.

CONTENTS

0

Your Circular Story

There are two ways of getting home;
and one of them is to stay there.
The other is to walk 'round the whole world
till we come back to the same place.

—G. K. Chesterton

The beginning of one of the most confusing, frightening, and frustrating seasons of my life started with a phone call.

Had I known that call would lead to me moving my family to Mexico, having our home broken into (and me angrily tracking down the dangerous thieves), having our lives threatened by a gang leader I ticked off, outrunning corrupt cops in a high-speed chase, and ultimately escaping all that chaos to start a cafe in the Andes Mountains of South America, I probably never would have answered the phone.

That's the story I'm going to tell in this book—that horrible season of my life. It was a season I wouldn't have wished on anyone.

Sounds inspiring, right?

For years, that season left me baffled. It felt like a setback.

I once heard a joke about a guy who walked out his front door and saw a snail on the porch. He picked it up, looked at it, then threw it across the yard. A year later, that same man heard a knock on his door. He opened it but didn't see anyone. He looked down and saw a snail.

The snail looked up at him and said in a squeaky voice, "What was that all about?"

I was that snail, and the man at the door was God.

I was left asking, "What in the world was that year of my life all about?!"

I'm gonna tell you the whole story of that wild year, but before we start, let's talk about you.

I know you've had a few seasons of life when you felt like a snail that got tossed across the yard. You've had painful experiences you never saw coming—relational struggles, divorce, illness, financial problems, and all sorts of personal battles. You were doing your best to live right and be faithful, but right in the middle of it, chaos struck and threw you into a season of just trying to survive. It took everything you had just to get back to where you started before the turmoil hit. You might be in the middle of trying to crawl back to where you started from right now. I'm also guessing you have your fair share of questions directed at Heaven.

Why did it have to end that way?

Why did they leave?

Why didn't God do something?

Why is this happening?

Did God allow this because He's mad at me?

Why, why, why?

When life punches us in the face, it's natural to ask why. We all want some sense of meaning and purpose. We want to understand why what's happening is happening. We know that if we can understand just a little—find some meaning or purpose—it will help us get through the difficult times.

In some way, every great religion and philosophy of the world is an attempt to explain the pain and suffering we experience in life and give some meaning to it. Pain is a human universal. Jesus said, "In this world you'll have suffering." Buddha said, "Life is suffering." We all have pain. If you think you don't have any pain, you're ignoring it. We all face pain, and deep down, we want to make some sense of it. We want to know why.

After working with lots of people as a counselor and leadership coach (and working through my own whys), I've concluded that the question—"Why?"—isn't the best one to ask in the middle of your pain. The better question is, *How am I going to respond to this?*

Why is for later. How is for now.

The answers to *why* usually only appear when looking backward, from further down the road of life. In the words of Søren Kierkegaard, "Life is lived forward but can only be understood looking backwards." If you're asking *why* in the middle of the pain, it can quickly lead to despair and hopelessness, because there's a good chance there isn't a good answer right now. The answers will only come later with the perspective of hindsight.

Pain and suffering tend to lead to shortsighted thinking. We get so focused on removing the pain that we lose sight of anything other than the things that promise to eliminate it. But when we can get some higher perspective on our situation, it can make all the difference. In the words of Viktor Frankl, "In some way suffering ceases to be suffering the moment it finds its meaning."[1] When we feel there's a purpose, it's a lot easier to hold onto faith and feel we'll find our way forward. That's my goal with this book. I want to help you get a bigger perspective on everything that has happened to you. I want to help you see that God really has been up to something big. There's an end goal in mind for everything you are facing, have faced, and will face.

Starting at the End

Before I send any book I've written to the editor, I first send the manuscript to my longtime mentor Karen. She and her husband, David (who, incidentally, play a huge part in the wild story I'm about to tell you), always shoot me straight. If they don't agree with something I've written, they'll tell me. But Karen has a weird quirk when it comes to reading my books: She always reads them backward. She starts with the last chapter, then works her way back to the first. I keep this in mind whenever I'm writing a book, because I know that if the end isn't good, I'll hear about it right away.

As I was outlining this book, I realized that starting from the end is actually the best way to begin. What I'm about to share should be the grand finale that I save for the end. But I'm going to start with it (sorry, Karen) since I want this book to serve as a roadmap for where you're heading.

So here's the end of the book: when life doesn't make sense, you can be certain that God is in the process of giving you a mission and a message that give you a deep sense of meaning and purpose.

In Romans 8:28, Paul boldly tells us: "And we know that in all things God works for the good of those who love him, who have been called according to his purpose." In the lead up to that encouraging line, he says, "I consider that our present sufferings are not worth comparing with the glory that will be revealed in us."[2]

In another of his letters he said, "So, we do not lose heart...this light momentary affliction is preparing for us an eternal weight of glory beyond all comparison."[3] He was encouraging his readers that you can be confident—no matter what comes—that God is working on something glorious.

Saint Irenaeus was talking about this truth when he said: *Gloria Dei est vivens homo*. This is often translated as, "The glory of God is man fully alive." God created us to be a reflection of his glory. When we're living out our mission, we're walking in that glory. But it doesn't end there. We're called to share the message of his unique work in our lives. When life doesn't make sense, you can be certain that God is in the process of taking everything that has happened in your life and using it for a purpose. I hope this book can serve as a roadmap to help you find that meaning and purpose.

This book has three key premises:

1. God is always at work in your life, but most of the time you can't see it or understand it.
2. God's work tends to follow a specific, circular pattern in every season of life. When we understand the pattern of His work, it helps us gain perspective on His divine hand in our life.
3. God's work in your life has prepared you with a unique message to share and a problem to solve that will point people to His goodness and, in the process, will give your life meaning and purpose.

God has a destiny for you. You are His "workmanship created in Christ Jesus for good works, which God prepared beforehand, that [you] should walk in them."[4] This is a book about how to connect the dots of His work in your life—even the seemingly random seasons that just don't make sense right now. It may have all felt random and chaotic, but right in the middle of it, there was a thread of purpose God was weaving into your story.

But God's work doesn't happen in a linear fashion. In fact, I've found that you can only get a really good perspective on His work in your life when you begin to see it in terms of a circle.

Let me explain.

Circular Paths of Righteousness

For most of human history, people have looked at time as a circle. Philosophers call it *eternal return*. Stoics called it *palingenesis*. Some cultures have depicted it as a snake in a circle, eating its tail. There's been an understanding that history tends to have patterns that repeat over long stretches of time. King Solomon put it this way: "What has been is what will be, and what has been done is what will be done, and there is nothing new under the sun."[5]

It wasn't until the last few hundred years, after the Enlightenment, that we decided time was some sort of straight line of progress. But that way of thinking wasn't the norm through most of history. Most of the non-Western world sees things in terms of a circle. (And, for the record, the Bible was written by people who had a non-Western perspective.) I think the people who saw time as a circle were onto something.

More importantly, I think God's work in our lives tends to look more like a circle than a straight line.

If you think back over your life, there are some themes, time frames, and places that you always seem to end up circling back to. They've been a consistent part of your history. You find yourself thinking, "This again?" or "Here again? I never thought I'd be back here." Because you've changed, each time you come back to those themes, locations, or ideas, they're familiar, but different—because *you* are different.

At our core, our personality, temperament, and giftings don't change. God made you who you are for a reason—even the parts of your physical appearance and personality that you don't like. Your personality and unique talents are gifts, placed in you by your Creator, that are never taken from you. Paul said it this way: "For the gifts and the calling of God are irrevocable."[6] He made you who you are for a very specific reason. He likes who He made. And He'll stop at nothing to make sure you become fully you.

God seems to have a very specific pattern to the way He leads us to becoming all He knows we can be.

In Psalm 23, the psalmist said our Shepherd leads us in "paths of righteousness." The Hebrew word used for path (*magol*) has a complex interpretation that means something closer to paths made of circles. Sheep tend to struggle to make it straight up a hill, so a shepherd leads them gently in circular paths—like a spiral—up the hill to where the good stuff is. Walking in circles typically brings negative images to mind. Who likes walking in circles? But what if walking in ever-widening circles is the way God gently guides us to where He wants to take us?

Carl Jung was tapping into this circular pattern of life when he said: "There is no linear evolution; there is only a circumambulation of the self."[7] You've been on a path, traveling around the core of who you are. At your core, you are still you. But God's love is changing you from the inside and pushing you outward. You're growing. Each time around the circle, you've been learning more about who you are and who you aren't. Expanding into your full potential. As you "work out your salvation with fear and trembling," like an ever-widening spiral, God is working "in you to will and to act in order to fulfill his good purpose."[8] You "are his workmanship, created in Christ Jesus for good works."[9] Paul talks about how "Christ's love compels us."[10] When the Spirit of God lives in you, His love naturally expands your capacity.

Every circle, every season of life, has taught you something new. It has expanded who you are. It has also prepared you with a unique message to share and problem to solve. Each circle has made you a little wiser, hopefully a little more humble, and a little more like Christ. God has been leading you on a journey to help you overcome your fear and doubt and begin to walk with faith that He is truly working all things together for your good. (If you don't believe me on that, then hopefully I'll convince you in the coming pages!) If you can keep that perspective, you'll be able to connect the dots and get a glimpse of God's hand at work in you.

And here's the really good news.

The struggles, challenges, and obstacles you're facing right now are all part of a circle—a season—in your life that you will look back at one day in awe. It will make sense. No matter how hard it is right now, if you can hold onto the perspective I want to share with you in this book, I believe something glorious is ahead. But oftentimes, to get that perspective, we need to look backward to look forward.

The Power of Your Story

Stories have power. Fairy tales and fables have been used from the beginning of time to connect us to timeless truths we need to thrive in this world. Stories communicate things we know on a deep, spirit level without realizing it. Stories have a way of connecting us to deep understanding that I don't believe we could process through just sharing knowledge or logic.

G. K. Chesterton concluded, "I had always felt life first as a story: and if there is a story there is a story-teller."[11] I believe with 100 percent confidence that God is always working behind the scenes in the world and in our lives. He is writing His story (or History) with your life.

And what makes a story good isn't random.

Every movie or tale we know and love has a very specific pattern. In fact, every story we love and connect with is basically the same, told with different characters and experiences.

Every great story—including yours—follows this pattern:

1. The Turning Point: A character is living their normal life, but they have a deep sense that there's more out there for them. Then an event happens that changes their life—an inciting incident that changes everything. Luke Skywalker meets two droids with a message. Dorothy is swept up in a tornado that takes her somewhere over the rainbow. Neo discovers the Matrix. Some major event changes the course of the character's life. Your story also has turning points—the birth of a child, a new job, getting fired, going

through a divorce, the loss of a loved one. That turning point changes everything. The change can be good or bad, but it always requires a level of courage to pursue the new adventure.

2. The Courage: The turning point creates chaos and uncertainty. The hero is forced to face their fears and be courageous. They have to decide they won't shrink back or run away. They boldly step forward, unsure of the outcome, but know they have to take on the adventure. They decide to face their fear and do it afraid.

3. The Guide: When the hero steps up with courage, a guide always appears to help them along the path—a figure like Obi-Wan Kenobi or Gandalf. In our lives, guidance may come through a friend, a book, a mentor, or a conversation that comes at a perfect moment. Jesus also promised He would leave us a guide who would lead us into all truth. When the student is ready, the teacher appears.

4. The Decision: The hero decides to step over the threshold and into the unknown. It's a whole new world filled with uncertainty and insecurity. But in committing to the path, the hero decides to be present and engage in the season. They commit to the path and a way opens to them. But the way is always fraught with challenges and struggles (aka adventure).

5. The Adventure: The hero is forced to face off with dragons, evil witches, or dark forces. In our lives, the struggles can appear as mental battles, wounds from the past, health struggles, relational challenges, and career difficulties. With each challenge the hero overcomes, they get stronger and wiser and discover potential they never realized they had within them.

6. The Dark Cave: The hero eventually faces a decisive battle against a force that threatens them. More often than not, the greatest battle is within themselves. They struggle with dark parts of

themselves and sometimes even with God and their beliefs about Him. Like Frodo choosing whether to use the ring for his own power or destroy it to save the world, every circle involves coming to grips with a side of us we'd rather not confront. The hero enters a dark cave, a dark night of the soul, and faces the dragon with courage.

7. The Resolution: They emerge from the dark cave victorious but often walking with a limp. They begin a journey back home, but they aren't the same as when they set out. They've been changed. They're a little more humble and wise. The resolution (or dénouement, as they call it in story writing) is a time for reflection and processing what just happened.

8. The New Perspective: The world looks different now. The hero's new perspective may feel awkward or make them feel out of place in the world. They see things through a new lens that has prepared them with a unique message to share and problem to solve.

9. The Message: The hero returns home with a message to share. If they've refused to get bitter or resentful about the journey, and if they've properly processed what happened, their story brings hope and courage to others.

Then, typically, a new adventure—a new circle—starts with a new turning point.

That's every story we love, in one form or another. And your story is no exception. At any given moment, your life is in one of those stages of the journey. Your story follows that circular pattern.

The shift from one stage of the journey to another isn't always black-and-white or clearly separated—it's a general pattern. But when you understand this pattern of God's work, it can help you gain perspective on what's happening, bring meaning and purpose to the journey you're on, and help you keep your eyes focused on the bigger picture in every season of life. I want this book to serve as a general roadmap for what to expect in each of those stages.

Now, I know right now you may be tempted to just jump ahead to the chapter that talks about the stage of the journey you feel describes your current situation—and that's fine. Go for it. Start there if you'd like. But then, I encourage you to jump back in and read the whole story, because that's really important. Each stage builds on itself and prepares you for what's ahead.

Your story is yours. But the message and perspective you've gained from each stage in your journey is something the world needs to hear. Sharing that message is your mission. It's your gift—a unique expression of God's redemptive work—to people fighting hard battles and asking their own *whys*.

So as we prepare to look at the story God has been writing in your life, let me ask you to consider a few things:

What if everything that has happened to you has prepared you for your greatest work?

What if all those seemingly random struggles and seasons have a divine purpose?

What if your unique struggles are important to the overall call in your life?

Right now, you may be at a turning point. Everything has changed, you know it, and it's leading to some major discomfort. Maybe you wanted a change, but this wasn't what you bargained for. If you're there, then I want to encourage you through this book.

Or it could be that you're right in the throes of the adventure. But it doesn't feel like an adventure—it feels like a giant mountain and you'll never get to the top. Know this: you are right in the middle of a circle. The struggles you are facing are making you stronger and preparing you for something ahead. Do your best to keep your perspective lifted and see that it's all preparation.

Or maybe you've just emerged from the fight of your life. You find yourself in a strange season of calm. It may feel weird. You might even feel a little guilty that things are going so well. Embrace this part of the circle. Reflect. As you read this book, look back at what you've just experienced and see if you can place the events in your life into their proper place in the circle. Take some time to slow down and consider the journey.

In this book, I'll tell the story of a crazy year of my life, and we'll unpack the framework I've been using as I counsel and coach people, help them launch businesses and ministries, write books, and step into new seasons of their lives. I'm going to share stories of people who discovered deep meaning and found their purpose by shifting their story into a message. We'll look at a guy who went on a mission trip for selfish reasons but ended up becoming obsessed with bringing clean water to people in Africa; he's now changing the lives of millions. We'll look at someone who wanted to be a missionary teacher but eventually became one of the top coffee experts in the world, improving the lives of coffee farmers around the globe. We'll look at someone who was the victim of cross-border human trafficking but, through a bizarre turn of events, actually ended up rescuing the people who sold him. We'll also look at the story of Jesus and see how His life fits the pattern of God's work. We'll see how each of these people's stories ultimately led them right to the destiny God had for them.

I've seen over and over again that your greatest work tends to emerge from the different seasons of preparation you've gone through. Often, it comes from your greatest struggle—the season you'd prefer just to leave out of your story.

I was actually writing a book on perspective when I went through the horrible season I'll tell you about in this book. But at the time, I had no perspective. I was too overwhelmed fighting with drug dealers and trying to stay alive to see the season for what it was—a circle that was expanding who I was. But now, in hindsight, I see the connection.

That first book I tried to write in Mexico never saw the light of day (thank heavens!). But now I'm writing the book I had no business writing back then. I see the connection. I'm convinced that, as you look back on your story, you'll be able to do the same. So, if you're ready, let's start connecting the dots so you can see how God has prepared you for your greatest work. Your best days are ahead.

I live my life in widening circles
that reach out across the world.
I may not complete this last one
but I will give myself to it.
I circle around God, around the primordial tower.
I've been circling for thousands of years
and I still don't know: am I a falcon,
a storm, or a great song?
—Rainer Maria Rilke

1

The Turning Point

The future is only the past again,
entered through another gate.

—*Arthur Wing Pinero*

It all started with a phone call.

Emily and I had been married for about six months when my friend David, a missionary in Mexico, called to tell me he and his wife, Karen (the lady who reads books backwards), were moving back to the United States. He asked, "Would you consider moving to Mexico to take over our ministry?"

I laughed. "Bro, that is *totally* not my calling."

"Yes, we agree. You are the least likely candidate, but we really feel like we're supposed to ask you."

Now, I'll admit. I had been feeling a bit restless. I had been serving as an associate pastor at a church for the past two years while getting my masters degree in counseling and was feeling a bit…well, bored. Before that season, I had been leading teams on four-month backpacking trips around the world. We'd fly one-way to Central America and work our way back to the U.S. border by land. Another trip had us going from Hong Kong up to Mongolia and out to far western China and Tibet. But I had put the back-packing on pause to get my graduate degree. And during that time, I also got married. A lot had changed in my life.

My pastoring job had been a blessing during that season of graduate school, but I was looking for a new adventure. Specifically, an international adventure. I was actually in the process of starting to lead week-long hiking trips with well-known national speakers on board to do leadership training for their fellow hikers (that group is called Summit Leaders). My first speaker had just signed on, and I was planning our first trip to Africa to climb Mount Kilimanjaro. Living on the coast of Mexico, at sea level, was not the international adventure I was looking for. In fact, it was the total opposite of what I wanted.

I had seen David and Karen's ministry and knew I had no busi-ness being down there. They worked in one of the roughest parts of Acapulco. The grandma next door to them was a drug dealer. Living next to her was a guy who everyone was pretty sure had killed two girls and left their bodies on the local basketball court, but no one could prove it. The guy down the street had shot a man multiple times, fled to the U.S. where he was arrested for another crime, then got deported back to Mexico. Somewhere in there some cops got paid off so he'd be left alone and free to roam the neighborhood. *Narcos* (drug cartels) had regular shootouts on the tourist beaches. They controlled most levels of government through bribes or just plain terror of what they might do if officials didn't comply with their corrupt demands.

David and Karen lived in this chaos. They were actually quite influential in the neighborhood, due to some pretty unorthodox "missionary-ing." At one point, David was attacked by one of the most dangerous dudes in the barrio. David is a giant of a man, so he promptly took him to the ground, then put him in a choke hold in front of the entire neighborhood. One guy who saw the incident told me, "We knew David was gonna kill him. But then he just got up and walked away." David kicked butt and took names—in Jesus's name, of course. He had led loads of people to Jesus in that insane neighborhood through some pretty wild tactics.

But me? I'm a skinny little white dude. I haven't been in a fight since elementary school. (And that didn't exactly go well for me.)

I knew I was not the right guy for the job. I had no desire to move to Mexico. But I had to be spiritual about it. So I said, "No. I don't think that's what God has for us."

But David insisted.

I knew that my only hope of getting out of the conversation was to drop the Christian trump card. So I finally said, "Let me pray about it."

That seemed to appease him, and he backed off. The call ended and I went on with my life, planning my outdoor expeditions.

But a few weeks later, David called back and asked, "Hey bro, what did you hear?"

"About what?"

He laughed. "Dude, you didn't even pray about it, did you?!"

Grr. Bad form, David. That's breaking the rules! When someone says, "I'll pray about it," that means: *Leave me alone!* You don't follow up and ask them if they actually prayed.

I confessed. "No, I...forgot."

"Dude...what does Emily think?" he asked.

Ugh. I hadn't told my wife. I knew she actually *would* pray about it. And I didn't want that. Plus, she was in Guatemala studying Spanish. She felt like she needed to improve her Spanish language skills for some things she thought might come in our future. (*Hmm...*I told myself it was purely coincidence.)

I agreed to tell Emily. And actually pray about it. And it all went downhill from there. That call was the turning point that started a ridiculously challenging season of my life.

And here's what I know about you: you may have never gotten a call to move to Mexico, but you've had quite a few turning points that changed everything in your life.

I'm guessing you can identify those key turning point moments pretty quickly. They come in all shapes and forms. Sometimes they're things we expected and wanted—marriage, the birth of a child, a job change. Sometimes they appear as things we never asked for.

I've talked to people from all walks of life, all over the world, and here are some of the turning points I've heard them share—some good, some not good:

- Parents getting a divorce
- Moving to a new city
- A miscarriage
- A life-threatening illness
- Loss of a loved one
- The first moment someone experienced something that became an addiction (alcohol, drugs, pornography)

- A mystical moment of connection with something "otherworldly"
- Divorce or separation
- Getting married
- Getting pregnant
- The birth of a child
- Adopting a child (and the process involved)
- Fostering a child
- Infertility
- Abandonment
- Betrayal
- Job changes (getting hired or fired)
- Reading a book that changed your perspective (which I hope this one will!)

All those turning points have one thing in common: change. A turning point is a defining moment that changes your life and sets you on a new journey.

I don't know many people who truly like change. Sure, we like it when it's on our terms. But typically, turning points force us to face life on terms we wouldn't have chosen for ourselves. We may have thought we knew what we were getting into, but often, the reality of the change is far more challenging than what we expected. (Getting married and having kids come to mind here!) When a turning point arrives, life changes in a significant way. It may come as a jolt, or it may be a slow realization, but at some point, we wake up and face a new reality. We realize that life is changing.

You Are Here

If you picked up this book, I'm guessing that right now your life probably fits roughly into one of these two categories:

A. You feel fairly content, even happy, with your life. You've got some challenges, but overall, life is pretty good. You love your family, have a good job, and your needs are met. But deep down, you still feel a little unfulfilled. You feel there's more in you. There are parts of you that aren't being used. You want to figure out how to activate and reach the potential you feel inside. Or:

B. You're facing a major life challenge right now—a medical diagnosis, a divorce, addiction, a loss. You're fighting a hard battle. You're trying to find God in the middle of this. Something deep within you says there's some sort of purpose to be found, but it's hard to see it right now. You want some hope that there really can be a happy ending and some meaning to all this suffering.

I've talked to highly successful CEOs at the top of their game who feel bored and know there's something more out there for them. They spend hours researching options online, checking out different jobs, maybe looking into a completely new career path—culinary school, getting another degree. I've talked to mothers who love raising their children but feel they have even more to give. I've talked to addicts who have hit rock bottom, and every time they shoot up or open the bottle, something says, *I'm better than this*. But the pain they're trying to cover is so great that they can't get out of the cycle. I've known people fighting for their life against a medical diagnosis who have a strange sense, right in the middle of the pain, that they're supposed to start something new.

Whether life is good and you're at the top of your game, or you feel like you've hit rock bottom, in one form or another, we all feel there's more in us—something bigger that we're called to.

I believe that desire for more was put there by God.

God has a very specific call on your life. That call never goes away. "The gifts and the calling of God are irrevocable."[1] You were created for a specific purpose. There's a connection between the feeling that there's more in you and the destiny God has for you. There's nothing wrong with you for wanting more—God put that desire there.

Sometimes we feel guilty about it, though. Shouldn't we just be grateful and content with what we have? Yes, we should. But the fact that you're looking for more doesn't mean you aren't grateful and content. I believe that looking for more is a natural response to God's Spirit living in us.

We were made from love and for love. Love always expands and grows. When God's Spirit is within you, it's the most natural thing for it to push you to expand your boundaries and seek more. The desire to be more than you are now is a call God placed within you. You are not yet all that you could be—you are called to greater things.

We live in a world that says, "Accept yourself just as you are and you'll be happy." That sounds great, but it's only partial truth. You know you aren't all you could be—your own conscience tells you so. You know you. And I know me. We know there's more to us than what we are now. We know we fall short of all the glory God intended for us.

Which is where Jesus comes in. He makes us acceptable. You can only accept who you are when you recognize that Jesus paid the price for what you, by nature, are not. He gained you total acceptance from God. When you start from that place—who you are because of Christ—you're on firm footing. Apart from that acceptance, you'll never drum up the ability to accept who you are without lying to yourself.

But when you accept Christ's gift, it creates a strange paradox of faith. In Christ, we are totally accepted, right now. God will never love us more than He does now. But that's just the start. That love and acceptance pushes us to reach our fullest potential in Christ.

The Apostle John talks about this process when he says, "Beloved, we are God's children now, and what we will be has not yet appeared."[2] We start the journey from our place of acceptance in Christ but, in the words of Jordan Peterson, "Never sacrifice what you could be for what you are now."[3] What you could be has yet to be seen. You have the potential to grow into the fullness of all God placed in you. It's a holy discontentment that drives us to be all God made us to be.

When you start your journey based in the security and confidence of your salvation, it leads you to do some pretty bold and adventurous things. The Apostle Paul talks about this when he says, "If we are 'out of our mind,' as some say, it is for God; if we are in our right mind, it is for you. For Christ's love compels us."[4] That verse can be a bit confusing depending on the translation you read. In some versions, the word "compels" is translated as "constrains," which seems like a contradiction. The Greek word Paul used is synechei, which carries the sense of God's love wrapping around you but then squeezing you in a way that pushes you out—like squeezing a tube of toothpaste. God's love surrounding you pushes you to become all you were made to be. When He pours His love into us, it pushes us to start doing things that might look a little crazy. People will see what His love compels us toward and say things like:

"Are you crazy? People like you don't do things like that."

"Who do you think you are?"

"Why on earth would you give up this to go do that?"

Only God knows the full potential He placed in us, and He knows exactly what it will take to get us to that place. And most of the time, the journey to that potential looks nothing like what we would choose for ourselves.

When David asked me to move to Mexico, I'll admit I was looking for something more—for an adventure. But the adventure that arrived at that turning point looked nothing like what I had expected or hoped for, so I wrote it off. Little did I know how important what was about to happen would be in the long-term plan God had for me.

The same will be true for you when your turning point arrives: It probably won't be what you expected or would have thought you wanted. You'll have to keep your perspective lifted to see what is happening—a new season is beginning.

The Inciting Incident

When I was eleven years old, my father announced that he was about to ruin my life. He didn't actually say it that way, but that's what I heard when he called us all into my sister's room and announced, "Your mother and I feel like God is calling our family to move to Guatemala in Central America."

I was devastated.

All I knew about Guatemala was the starving kids, shacks, and poverty I had seen in the pictures my parents had brought back from a previous trip there. I also knew the country was embroiled in a brutal civil war where it was hard to tell the good guys from the bad guys—there were atrocities on all sides. For all I knew, we'd be living in a bombed-out shack eating scraps of food from a garbage dump. On top of that, my middle school social life was just starting to take off. I was now sitting with the cool kids at lunch, and I was getting more confident on the baseball diamond. This would ruin all of that. I protested vehemently, but a few months later we boarded a plane and moved to Central America.

That moment was a huge turning point. Not only did it start a new season, it changed the entire course of my life. And, as I would discover with my call to go to Mexico many years later, it would make international missions part of my life's repeating circles.

Every great adventure—every circle—starts with a turning point. Indiana Jones finds a clue that will lead him on an adventure to find the Ark of the Covenant. Jason Bourne wakes up with no memory and has to discover who he is. Sometimes the character in the story or movie is a reluctant hero. Sometimes he or she willingly embraces the unknown. But either way, the turning point is where the action starts. In fact, movie- and fiction-writing experts tell you that if you want to keep people engaged, the inciting incident (aka turning point) needs to happen early in the story. The conflict that changes the character's life has to start quickly, because we love watching conflict (other peoples' conflict, anyway). Conflict is what grabs our attention and locks us in.

Within a few shorts weeks of my family moving to Guatemala, I was jolted awake by an earthquake in the middle of the night. Guatemala sits on a huge fault line, so it's filled with active volcanoes and smaller fault lines. We all scrambled outside into the street when we realized what was happening. I had never experienced anything like that, and it was pretty nerve-racking. Once the shaking stopped, we made our way back to our rooms and went to bed, but I couldn't sleep after that. Over the next several days there were regular aftershocks that left me feeling unbalanced and wobbly. I felt like I couldn't even trust the ground under my feet. On top of the shaking, the active volcanoes became even more active, spewing out lava and ash that would darken the sun. It all felt very apocalyptic. I was kind of freaking out. Was the world coming to an end?

I remember expressing my concern about the earthquakes and volcanoes to a missionary who had been living in Guatemala for over thirty years. He was unfazed. "Oh, that's just because seasons are changing. There's always some shaking when the seasons change." I learned that Guatemala has a dry season and a rainy season. When the seasons are about to shift, the volcanoes become more active and there are lots of tremors.

I think that's a pretty good picture of how most season changes happen in our lives. Our world starts shaking. The turning point leaves us feeling like we can't even trust the ground under our feet anymore. Everything looks different and cloudy. Sometimes we wonder if it's the end of the world. But it's not. (I'm pretty certain it will be *really* clear when it's the end of the world.)

If the ground is shaking around you and everything feels pretty uncertain right now, don't be afraid. Just start paying attention. It's part of the circular nature of God's work. Do your best to keep perspective on what all the shaking is—a turning point that starts a new season.

When a turning point arrives, it's common for the hero to avoid the change or reject the call to adventure it brings. They try to hold on to what's familiar. Luke Skywalker told Obi-Wan he couldn't rescue the princess because he had to help his uncle with the harvest. When Saul was anointed as king of Israel, he ran and hid at first. As much as they may be discontent with their current life, the idea of everything changing leads to lots of fear and discomfort in the hero-to-be. Turning points are uncomfortable, so we tend to run from them.

The COVID-19 pandemic became a turning point for many people as it shook up their routine. For some, it compounded discomfort they had been able to avoid up to that point with the busyness of life. But when they were forced to slow down, it brought everything into stark clarity. Some people flipped out and started panicking. They tried to numb themselves of the discomfort and fell into self-destructive habits.

But others saw it as a chance to make a needed change. They started moving all over the country (and world). Others changed jobs. Some got out of toxic relationships or job situations. And lots of babies were born—a major turning point in life! If anything good came of the pandemic (God loves to redeem even the worst of situations), it may have been how much the discomfort became a turning point for many people to step out and change their lives. Many actually stepped into their calling for the first time. The turning point is uncomfortable, but it can become a catalyst for getting you right where you need to be if you respond to it correctly.

The Gift of Discomfort

When Dave asked me to move to Mexico, I had been feeling pretty uncomfortable at my current job. I felt underutilized. I felt like I was just filling in gaps where no one would step up. The monotony of the job, while great during the time I was in grad school, was starting to drive me bonkers. Discomfort is a hallmark of a turning point, but it's also pretty common to feel discomfort with our lives leading up to the turning point.

My dad describes the discomfort that leads to a turning point as a time when "the grace has lifted." God gives us specific grace to deal with the challenges of each season of life and help us get through all the frustrations and annoyances. It's like grease that helps reduce friction and irritation. But when a season begins to change, God will often lift the specific grace we needed for that season. Obviously, God never lifts His complete grace off humanity, but He seems to shift His grace to prepare us for what's to come, and little irritations we used to overlook now really annoy us. Frustrations we could handle before begin to feel unbearable. I think the discomfort we feel before a turning point is a gift, because it helps us loosen our attachment to our current circumstances in preparation for what's to come.

We naturally take the path of least resistance in life. Oftentimes, we won't change anything until the pain of staying the same is greater than the pain of moving into the unknown. Pain can be a gift that way. No normal person likes pain. But often God will use pain and discomfort to push us to where we need to be.

When a mother eagle knows it's time for her baby eagles to learn to fly, she starts pulling the soft feathers out of the nest so the babies feel the sticks beginning to poke them. The nest is comfortable, but eagles are made to fly. So the mother does whatever it takes to get those birds out there, soaring high. God does the same for us.

Comfort tends to be the enemy of reaching your destiny. Comfort will keep you from moving forward. I've seen that God will often give the gift of discomfort right before a transition is about to happen. Discomfort is a good sign that it might be about time for you to jump out of the nest and start to fly.

It can be difficult to know whether the discomfort is telling you something truly needs to change or whether you need to shift your perspective on your current situation. That's why we'll talk about the guide who always appears to help give direction in each circle in an upcoming chapter. But for now, know this: You will know when the right opportunity arises. It will be clear. Usually, the clearest sign that you need to pursue an adventure is the fact that it looks nothing like you expected it would and it scares you.

Identifying Your Turning Points

I recently asked my wife what she thought were three of the major turning points in her life. She mentioned a moment in college when she was at a wild party and realized just how out of place she felt. She loves a good time, but she knew this wasn't the kind of good time she was made for. A friend of hers even came up and told her, "You don't belong here. Let me take you home." It wasn't some major, life-altering event for her. It was more a moment of realization and clarity. She knew she was called to *not* fit in. She was called to be different.

The inciting incident isn't always dramatic, with clouds parting and doves descending. Sometimes it's just a moment when things click in your mind and you start to see how different you are from those around you in some way. Those moments of internal understanding can be just as life-altering as an external crisis.

Emily has connected the dots between that moment and an ongoing theme in her life—hospitality. Because she knows what it's like not to fit in with the normal crowd, she's always on the lookout for those who may be feeling lonely or out of place. She has felt her own loneliness and sense of not fitting in, so she looks for people she can make feel welcome in any environment in which she finds herself. When she goes to events, even ones she's not in charge of, she will often just start hosting and connecting people. Even as a teen, her struggle was pointing to her destiny as a person who pays attention to those who feel out of place.

Your story will be no different. When you identify the moments that changed you, you'll start to see some consistent themes and get some perspective on your unique calling. You can start connecting the dots. The inciting incidents in your life hold deep truth if you'll listen to them.

So let's start there.

What would you say was the most recent turning point in your life? A moment that changed your life significantly?

Now, look back a little further. What was the turning point prior to that?

As you look back, you'll notice that some turning points are wonderful experiences. Some aren't. But either way, they set you on a new path.

If you're at a turning point right now, you have a choice to make. You'll have to decide how to respond. Two paths are in front of you. One path leads to frustration and anxiety. The other can lead to meaning and purpose.

Let me explain.

Will You Embrace the Adventure?

When the turning point appears, or an inciting incident forces you into change, you'll have to decide how you'll look at your situation. Whether a situation limits you or propels you forward tends to depend on the lens through which you look at it. You can see yourself in one of two ways:

1. **A Victim.** You didn't sign up for this. You thought your spouse would be faithful to the end. You thought you'd always have your health. You thought you were indispensable at your job. But you were wrong. It's not fair what happened. You were victimized. It's easy to sit around and moan and complain about the situation. The problem is, most of life comes down not to what happens to you, but to how you interpret what has happened to you—your perspective. If you focus on how you were victimized, your brain will immediately shift into survival mode. You'll be on edge, constantly watching for threats to your security, connection, and sense of control. You'll eventually get angry, bitter, and resentful. This leads nowhere good and keeps you stuck.

So may I suggest another option? Why not see yourself as:

2. **An Adventurer.** In the words of G. K. Chesterton, "An adventure is only an inconvenience rightly considered. An inconvenience is only an adventure wrongly considered."[5] You didn't sign up for this, but it is what it is. Yes, it's scary and overwhelming. You didn't think life would look like this, but you've faced hard things before and made it through—and you're stronger for it. So bring it on!

When you choose to see yourself as a willing participant in an adventure—rather than a victim—your brain chemistry actually begins to shift. Your mind goes into exploration-and-learning mode, rather than fear. You didn't choose the adventure, the adventure chose you—but you're willingly confronting what is ahead as an adventurer. You aren't a victim. You are an adventurer. That small perspective shift can change everything.

You will never avoid the turning points in life. They're going to come, one way or another. It's up to you to decide how you will face them.

May I suggest you begin to see yourself as a brave adventurer?

I've seen a lot of people make their life a lot harder because they resist moving into the adventure. They try to run and hide. They try to ignore the fact that life has changed. They fight hard and push back. They get frustrated and depressed trying to hold on to some semblance of what life used to be before the inciting incident. I believe God will always complete His work in us, but we can make it more difficult by choosing to reject or run from the call out of fear. The turning point—the call to adventure—will always come with fear. It's natural and normal. But that doesn't mean you should run from it. More often than not, the life you really want is on the other side of the thing you fear most.

So let's talk about how to face the fear that comes with the adventure.

2

The Courage

*Courage is almost a contradiction in terms. It means a
strong desire to live taking the form of a readiness to
die.... A soldier surrounded by enemies, if he is to cut
his way out, needs to combine a strong desire for living
with a strange carelessness about dying. He must seek
his life in a spirit of furious indifference to it; he must
desire life like water and yet drink death like wine.*

—G. K. Chesterton

After David's second call asking us to consider going to Mexico,
I finally told Emily about his very unappealing offer. She
prayed and, as I feared, felt we needed to at least check it out. (That's
exactly why I hadn't told her!) So we booked tickets to Acapulco for
a scouting trip right after she got back from Guatemala.

The visit confirmed all my worst fears about the place. It was
the total opposite of what I had envisioned for our future. I
wanted to be climbing mountains in the fresh, crisp air. This
would be sea-level living in the heat and humidity. Worse yet, the
neighborhood was getting even more dangerous as *narcos* (drug

traffickers) were trying to take control of the area. There were police checkpoints all over town with Special Forces operators with machine guns, wearing balaclavas to protect their identity, and open shootouts on the beach, even in tourist areas, between rival gangs and *narcos*.

David and Karen gave us the lowdown on all the people in the neighborhood to watch out for—the guy who sold drugs, the one who had most likely killed two girls and gotten away with it, the most dangerous and volatile gang member in the hood. (Pro tip: if you're trying to convince someone to move to a place they're already hesitant about, don't go telling them all the horrible realities around them!) The place was way worse than I even thought it was. I love a challenge, but this actually scared me.

When we got back home and I had time to process everything, I was even more hesitant than before we went. The decision probably would have been easier had we not seen the reality of the situation before we went. For the record, sometimes it's best to go in blind, without too much information. But when you have the information about what's ahead, it will still usually come packaged in lots of fear. Fear of the unknown. Fear of loss. Fear of potential danger. Fear of looking foolish.

If you're at a turning point and don't have any fear, there's a good chance you don't know all the details or you're ignoring facts. The decision to face the fear and anxiety will define whether you stay living in a small circle of fear or start the adventure into a whole new world. Fear is natural in the face of the unknown. But you'll have to get comfortable with facing off with your fear. Fear never goes away, but you can learn how to free yourself from its grip. Believe it or not, the only way to break free from fear is to face the thing you fear—head on, in small doses.

Life Is Dangerous

One of the most popular hikes I lead is a thirty-mile trek walking where Jesus walked in Israel. We hike from Nazareth to Zippori (a city Jesus most likely helped build), stay in an Orthodox Jewish kibbutz, go up over the Horns of Hattin (the site of an infamous Crusader battle) and Mount Arbel, down to Galilee, and up to the Mount of Beatitudes, where we spend the night at the Franciscan abbey there. It's quite an adventure!

When I first started doing these trips, I would get loads of emails from potential hikers asking, "Is it safe?"

I got so overwhelmed with people asking this question that I created a front page to the application with questions and answers. Here's what part of the first page looks like:

———

IMPORTANT: Please read this entire page of FAQ's before you sign up for this trip.

Is Israel safe?

Life is inherently dangerous. Because you will be alive while on this trip, there is an element of risk involved. There are some steep downhill sections and the hike is challenging. Not to mention…politics. An Israeli friend of mine once told me, "Israel is a peaceful nation. Everyone wants a piece of us." Violence can erupt at any time in Israel. In the event of severe danger, we will cancel the trip...That said, millions of people visit Israel each year and come back to tell about it. Tourism is a cash cow, particularly in the area of Galilee where we will be hiking, so it's generally a peaceful area...Israeli peaceful.

I know I've probably scared off some wonderful, loving people with the blunt (and somewhat sarcastic) answers on that warning page. But the fact is, this hike requires a level of physical and emotional commitment that is way beyond a walk through a local park. There is risk. I need people who have evaluated the risk and decided it's worth taking. Things may get a little intense. One year while we were hiking, the U.S. president took out a top Iranian leader and Iran threatened to retaliate against Israel. Our whole team was getting texts from people back home warning us that World War III was about to start right where we were. Obviously, it didn't. But who knows? It could have. But if you want to see Israel, that's the reality you have to face.

The same is true for life. If you want the adventure, you have to embrace the risk.

Life is full of danger and threats and scary things that go bump in the night. Nobody is getting out alive. We may feel secure or safe because we've reduced our life to a level where we don't have to face anything we fear—but that security is an illusion. It just means it will eventually show up in your nice, safe little world and shock you.

Living with an element of risk is part of living a fulfilling and purpose-filled life. Another weird paradox of our faith is that you only get the experience of truly living when you're willing to surrender yourself to the possibility of death. "For whoever wants to save their life will lose it, but whoever loses their life for me will save it."[1] Way too many people never really live because they're trying to arrive safely at death.

Faith requires courage.

Every new season will require a new level of faith and courage. You'll have to step out into the unknown with no guarantee of the outcome. But here's what I've discovered through facing my own fears: you have no idea what is waiting on the other side of your willingness to be courageous.

Fear tends to cause us to sacrifice the potential within us. We settle for what is, because what *could be* involves risk. But the life you really want is usually on the other side of stepping into the unknown.

I'll make a bold statement here. I don't believe you can live a full, God-honoring life without taking some God-honoring risks. God-honoring risks show the world you have hope in something greater than yourself, money, or your own strength and intelligence. It shows we trust our life is in God's hands and He wants what's best for us. It shows we really have faith in His ability to make all things work together for the good of those who love Him. It shows we truly believe He is leading us in every season and circle along the way.

The journey of faith is a journey of overcoming fear and taking risks. As Joseph Campbell said on many occasions, "The cave you fear to enter holds the treasure that you seek."[2] The path of the righteous is like the light of dawn that shines brighter and brighter. But to get to the dawn, you always have to face the fear and courageously move into the dark unknown.

The Faces of Fear

I met with a guy awhile back who was a high-ranking officer in the military. He was about to retire and was trying to figure out his next phase of life. He told me he had no idea what he wanted to do next. After working with lots of people in transition, I've found that when someone says they don't know what they want to do next, it tends to be a sign of fear. They actually do know, but there's fear involved, so they avoid it by saying they don't know what they want. I shared that with him.

He straightened up in his seat. "Oh, I'm not afraid." He talked about dangerous and risky situations he had faced serving all over the world.

I pushed a little more. "Surely, there's something you've been thinking you might want to do."

He shook his head. After talking a few minutes longer, he said, "Well, I am interested in going back to college." He paused. "But I'd be the oldest guy in the classes. I haven't taken a test in years."

I smiled. "So, are you worried you wouldn't be able to keep up with the young people and the rigors of school?"

"No. I'm not worried. It's just . . ."

We went back and forth for quite some time with him refusing to acknowledge that he had some "concerns"—aka fears. We left the conversation with him still unsure about what he wanted to do next, mostly because he didn't want to acknowledge his fear.

Anxiety, worry, concern, avoidance, you name it—they're all faces of fear. I've seen lots of people fail to move forward because of fear, but they don't recognize it as fear. They call it uncertainty or caution or say, "The timing isn't right." But ignoring fear doesn't make it go away. Fear thrives in the dark and gets bigger. If we don't acknowledge and face our fear, it comes out in weird ways.

Here are a few ways fear shows up in our lives that keeps us from moving forward:

1. **Analysis Paralysis.** In the name of preparation (which I'm totally in favor of, by the way), many people research, study, and analyze themselves out of the adventure. Unlimited information on the internet, TV, and social media has paralyzed them. They've listened to the experts (especially the ones who confirm their fears). They've weighed every possible variable and concluded the risk is just too great. There's too much to lose—financially, relationally, or reputationally. So they don't move forward and they get stuck. They stay in their small, limited circle of fear. Eventually, playing it safe leads to feeling disappointed with the world and, ultimately, with themselves. It makes you cynical and resentful of others who have taken the risk and pursued their dreams. It can also lead to lots of regret, wondering what could have been. Google and research all you want, but there are some answers a search engine will never have. Those answers can only be found by courageously stepping out into the unknown. As Reinhard Bonnke once said, "Those who forever seek the will of God are overrun by those who do it."

2. Feeling Unqualified/Disqualified. When I first started leading outdoor adventures, I would regularly get emails from people asking me what qualifications I had to be leading people in the wild. I'd get really insecure about it, because I have zero qualifications or certifications in outdoor stuff. I just like being outdoors and watching what happens when people go there. I'm not qualified, but I'm doing it! Interestingly, I'd usually find out those people were actually asking me for a job! They wanted to do what I was doing and thought *they* needed some sort of certification. Funny how that works...The brave become leaders.

Too many people spend their entire life in perpetual training—getting more education, reading more books. They never actually do the thing they're preparing for because they think they need one more qualification in order to be ready. I'm totally in favor of education and training, but if you're waiting around for the right person to "certify" you, there's a good chance you'll never get started. You have to just step into the adventure and learn along the way.

When people saw the boldness of the apostles at Pentecost, many of whom were just fishermen, they realized what set them apart was that they had been with Jesus. We're all unqualified, but Jesus qualifies us. Jesus paid the price so you could be courageous. You've probably heard it before: God doesn't call the qualified, He qualifies the called.

Don't let lack of training or past mistakes convince you that you are disqualified from a call. That is a lie. If being messed up or not certified disqualified you from doing something of value, we'd all be disqualified. In fact, pretty much every character in the Bible would be disqualified.

3. Fear of Looking Foolish or Failing. When you're worried about losing your reputation and being in a position that makes you feel vulnerable, it will keep you from ever stepping into something new. I hate to break it to you, but that fear is a sign of pride. Pride is a weird thing. It can appear as arrogance or fear—at the same time and in the same person. Some of the most arrogant people I know are also the most fearful. Pride tells you to keep things under your control and look like you have it all together. But stepping into the unknown tends to leave you vulnerable and can make you look foolish. Courage requires a willingness to look foolish. As G. K. Chesterton put it: "Anything worth doing is worth doing badly."[3] Sometimes you have to start out doing something badly. You might even need to fail. But eventually, you'll learn and improve and be glad you tried.

4. Timing. The right time for an adventure often feels like the worst possible time. We get an idea in our minds about when we'll go for it—once we have more money saved, after the kids are in college, once we pay off the house, once the economy is a bit more stable. The opportunity is sitting right in front of us, but it comes with risk. It seems wise to wait. And sometimes it is wise to wait. But oftentimes, the call to an adventure of faith will appear before you feel ready or at the worst possible time.

When my dad moved our family to Guatemala, my brother and sister and I were all under age twelve. Guatemala was in the middle of a civil war. Nobody was sure who the good guys were and who the bad guys were. It was a really bad time. It would have been much safer to wait until we were older or until peace was declared. But he was courageous, and we reaped the benefits.

Sometimes, we don't step out because we feel it's too late. Our best days are behind. But the fact is, if you're still breathing, you still have a purpose and adventure to pursue. It's never too late.

5. Opposition. When you decide to step into the unknown, it's pretty common to get opposition from the very people you would expect to support you. You'll get negative feedback. They'll question your decisions or try to hold you back. Your willingness to move forward makes them uncomfortable. Some actually believe they want the best for you when they advise you against taking the journey. There are all sorts of motivations people have for keeping you where you are, but if you're feeling the call, you can't let the opposition hold you back. You'll have to get over your fear of other peoples' opinions. Listen to their advice and counsel; God often speaks through people, even enemies—but you must ultimately listen to the guide within you. (More on how to identify that voice in the next chapter.)

Whatever your fear may look like, here's the important thing to recognize about it: Fear doesn't go away. It must be acknowledged and faced; otherwise it becomes a constant impediment to your forward movement. You have to recognize the fear and face it wisely, in small doses. The more you face it, the more you become immune to its effects on you. You'll probably never become fearless, but you can fear less. That's how you conquer the fear and step into the adventure.

Transcending Fear

I wrote a book called *Love Slows Down* that talks about how all our hopes and dreams are wrapped up in seeking three things:

1. Security (emotional, physical, financial)
2. Connection (feeling valued, accepted, loved)
3. Control (a sense of empowerment and the ability to make our own choices)

Those three things aren't just the source of our greatest hopes and dreams. They're also the source of our anxiety and fear. Every fear we have comes from feeling a threat to one of those three things. Fear eventually leads to anger, so threats to those three things are also the source of our anger. When we feel anxiety, anger, frustration, or discomfort about something happening to us, it's always because of something happening inside us. It's because we feel a threat to our security, connection, or control.

Fear was the first, primal emotion felt by our ancestors when sin entered the world. Being separated from God's love—the only true source of security, connection, and control—Adam and Eve felt fear. We've all felt it, in one form or another, ever since. Fear is a driving force in every human, no matter how much we ignore it or act like it isn't there.

We all start our journey of faith driven by fear of not getting those needs met. But because Jesus has reconnected us to the perfect source of security, connection, and control—God's love—we don't have to be afraid anymore. I know it sounds super simplistic, like some lame greeting card, but we really do have all we need in God's love.

Confidence in that love gives us courage to move forward. But if we stay focused on our fear of not getting security, connection, and control, we end up not walking in the confidence that love gives us. We get stuck in a cycle of self-preservation. It can lead to self-absorption—living just to guard what we have. Fear makes your world small. It causes you to constantly focus on getting your needs met and run from anything that threatens those needs. When you live in fear, you never really live at all.

God made us with those needs and wants to be the source that meets them. That's why Jesus said if you want all of those things, you don't find them by seeking them—you find them by seeking something higher. "Seek first the kingdom of God and his righteousness, and all these things [security, connection, and control] will be added to you."[4] When you're focused on the highest possible perspective—God's Kingdom—it gives the courage and confidence to move forward. You stop looking at all that could go wrong and start looking at all that could go right. When you seek a higher aim and step out in courage, all the things you need will materialize.

Or you might step out in courage and die. And then all your problems really will be solved.

Just kidding, sort of. (But seriously, I doubt you'll die.) Here is something encouraging, though: Jesus actually did die when He surrendered to a higher call. But what came from that risk brought more life than anyone ever could have imagined. God will often ask you to do something that feels like dying, but when He brings resurrection from the death, there's no limit to how glorious the outcome may be. We have no idea what is possible when we surrender our life to the risks God asks us to take in our adventure of faith.

If it's worth doing, it will probably involve fear and uncertainty. It will require courage. Getting married takes courage. Having kids takes courage. Applying for a new job takes courage. Starting a business, confessing the addiction, etc., etc. I'm convinced that fear is usually a sign that's the direction you need to head. If it scares you, that's probably what you need to do.

The price of taking a risk is scary in the moment. But there are worse things. The only thing more uncomfortable than the anxiety about what might happen is the pain of looking back at what could have been.

I climbed Mount Elbrus in the Caucasus Mountains with a guy whose friend asked him to go in with him on buying a small sandwich shop with a weird name for just a few thousand dollars many years ago. The guy said it seemed too risky, so he turned down the offer. That sandwich shop became the Schlotzsky's sandwich chain. Ouch! Every big payoff tends to start with what seems to be significant risk at the time.

And you know this, because you've already had to make some courageous decisions to get to this point. If you look back over your life, you'll probably remember fears you had that seem silly now but seemed like the end of the world at the time. You may not have felt courageous, or you may have been forced into courage, but either way, you're here because you stepped out and moved forward into the unknown. You thought it was the end, but it wasn't. It was actually just the beginning. The same is true now. The life God has ahead for you is just on the other side of your greatest fears. You've already experienced the benefits of courage. Remember those benefits as you take the next step into the adventure.

Irrational Fear and Ultimate Fear

We had some pretty rational reasons for our fear about living in Acapulco. The place was dangerous. We had facts and evidence.

But oftentimes, fear is irrational. I've struggled with major fear my entire life. A lot of times that fear is irrational—and I know it. Well-meaning people will tell me, "Just look at the facts. Facts over fear." But the fact is, irrational fear isn't moved by rational facts, because it's, well…irrational. Fear is a strong, primal emotion. It's the first thing we felt when we fell short of the glory of God. So the only thing that will drive out fear is something stronger.

And there's one thing stronger than fear.

"There is no fear in love. But perfect love drives out fear."[5]

The only thing stronger than irrational fear is God's perfect love that offers security, connection, and empowerment/control. The greater our understanding of God's love poured out into our hearts,[6] the more His love compels us to courage.[7] Sometimes, you just have to do it afraid, walking in faith that God's love will hold you up in the struggle.

We conquer irrational fear with God's love by stepping out and doing what scares us, trusting that neither "height nor depth, nor anything else in all creation, will be able to separate us from the love of God in Christ Jesus our Lord."[8] You only get to test that love by stepping out and trusting He will take care of you.

Interestingly, Solomon said, "The fear of the Lord is the beginning of wisdom."[9] The fear of the Lord is a confusing thing that causes lots of people (including me, for years) to live with an unhealthy understanding of God. For those who have accepted the gift of salvation through Jesus, the fear of the Lord has a new meaning. The fear of the Lord is a healthy reverence for the fact that you're created for a purpose and have a mission to accomplish. When we stand before Him, we'll give account for what we did with the gift of life He gave us. Keeping that end in mind leads us to make courageous decisions in obedience to His call. Based on that obedience, we'll be rewarded accordingly.[10]

You may not feel that courageous when you're stepping out, but your feelings will follow your action. Remember, there's a bigger prize at stake here—an eternal prize. In the parable of the man who buried his talent,[11] Jesus seems to indicate that you only get credit when you step up and use what you have to the best of your ability. You don't get credit for good intentions or thinking courageous and noble thoughts. Watching movies about heroes, listening to inspirational gurus, and pumping your fist in the air to songs that amp you up isn't enough. You have to actually step out. Only action counts.

In the words of Theodore Roosevelt:

> The credit belongs to the man who is actually in the arena, whose face is marred by dust and sweat and blood; who strives valiantly; who errs, who comes short again and again, because there is no effort without error and shortcoming; but who does actually strive to do the deeds; who knows great enthusiasms, the great devotions; who spends himself in a worthy cause; who at the best knows in the end the triumph of high achievement, and who at the worst, if he fails, at least fails while daring greatly, so that his place shall never be with those cold and timid souls who neither know victory nor defeat.[12]

You have a call to fulfill. You're God's handiwork, created for a purpose.[13] Don't shrink back in fear, wondering what could have been. Step up and fulfill your destiny. Receive the reward of becoming all God intends for you to be.

Knowing When to Risk

I mentioned that my dad moved our family to Guatemala while the country was in the middle of a civil war. He got some pushback from well-meaning family and friends about this decision. It seemed reckless. As a forced participant in this adventure, I wasn't exactly thrilled about it either. But as I look back, I realize that move was the best possible thing my dad could have done for me. His courage was an example for me that has stuck with me throughout my life.

My dad spent a lot of time in prayer and seeking counsel before he moved us down there. But he wasn't ever 100 percent certain. Looking back, the long-term rewards for our family far outweighed the risk. But it doesn't always turn out this way. Sometimes people take the risk and pay a high price for it. Sometimes they even die. Which brings up a question: How do you know what risks to take?

When it comes to making these kinds of decisions, I'm convinced of one thing: There is no formula. There is only revelation. Each person must receive a direct revelation from God regarding what they must do.

Not every risk is something that needs to be pursued. But most great opportunities require some level of risk. As Roy Williams says: "Opportunity and security are inversely proportionate. As one increases, the other must decrease. High returns are gained from low-risk strategies only through the passage of time. He who will cheat time must embrace the risk of failure."[14] There's always a chance of failure. But there's also a chance that you could see results that are beyond your wildest dreams. Don't ignore the potential danger, but keep your perspective lifted on the potential benefits.

As a follower of Christ, you don't get to choose your adventure; God chooses it for you. But you do get to choose how you'll respond to the adventure. You get to choose to be courageous and trust that God is leading you somewhere good. Trust that God's plan for you is what your plan would be if you knew all the details.

So, let me ask you something: If you really believed that God was pleased with you and accepted you, then what would you pursue? If you really believed that "if God is for us, who can be against us,"[15] what would you do? If you really believed God was for you, how much could your life change? What courageous step do you need to take right now to move forward in this season?

The adventure will always require risk and courage. Taking risks always requires wisdom. Fortunately, we aren't asked to figure out our journey alone. In fact, every heroic journey into the unknown involves the insight of a guide. Which is what we'll talk about next.

Run from what's comfortable. Forget safety.
Live where you fear to live.
Destroy your reputation. Be notorious.
I have tried prudent planning long enough.
From now on I'll be mad.

—*Rumi*

The Guide

When the student is ready, the teacher will appear.

—*Ancient proverb*

When we got home from our exploratory trip to Mexico, for the first time, I actually started praying about what we were supposed to do. My plans for leading the outdoor adventure trips were still on track, so I didn't want to jeopardize that dream by taking on another commitment. If moving to Mexico really was something God had in His plans for me, I needed a clear sign.

Based on a previous experience, I knew God was able to give exactly the kind of sign I needed. Just two years earlier, on the same day I had asked Emily's dad for permission to marry her, I got a phone call from Karen (yes, the Karen who reads books backwards and wanted us to move to Mexico.) I hadn't talked to her in months, but she said, "Hey Joël, I felt like I was supposed to call and tell you the timing is wrong on something you're about to do."

I told her I had just asked permission to marry Emily. "Is that what you're talking about? Am I supposed to wait on that?" I asked.

"I don't know. I just felt like I was supposed to tell you that."

I kept quizzing her for details. "What else did God tell you?"

But she just said I needed to pray about what to do with what she'd shared.

I wasn't exactly happy about receiving this call; I wanted to move forward. I had gotten up all this courage to propose, I asked Emily's dad's permission, and I had already bought a ring—now I was being told I might be about to make a mistake. I was confused.

To top it all off, the following morning, another mentor called and basically said the same thing: the timing is wrong. The mentor didn't give details. But the message was pretty clear—I wasn't supposed to marry Emily, yet.

Since I had told her dad and others that I was going to propose, but didn't, the next few months were really awkward. How do you tell a dad, "I'm pretty sure God told me *not* to marry your daughter…" Thank heavens Emily waited and didn't give up on me. Loads of people accused me of being afraid of commitment, but I really felt like I had a clear sign.

It ended up being another entire year before I felt a peace about asking her to marry me. During that year, a series of really crazy things happened that, I now realize, would've started our marriage off on really shaky footing. God needed to work some things out of me and prepare us both for marriage.

Based on that experience, I knew God could make things clear about moving to Mexico. And I knew better than to listen to Karen on this one. She was biased!

So I asked for a sign.

Actually, I asked for several signs. And, as I'll tell you about shortly, I got my signs—all of them! I got clear direction that we were supposed to move to Mexico.

Because every new circle is a new adventure, it comes with a need for clarity and direction. Sooner or later, maybe even right now, you find yourself looking at the possibilities and options ahead and asking:

Is this really what I'm supposed to do?

How do I know which path to take?

How do I prepare for what's ahead?

What will the journey be like?

If we're the first person in our family or circle of friends to step out and do this kind of thing, we have no model to follow. It all feels wild and new. We feel completely unprepared and unqualified. Even after we choose to move forward in spite of fear, there are a lot of unknowns.

Fortunately, in every great story, a guide appears to help the hero on the journey. Think Gandalf, Morpheus, or Dumbledore. Sometimes the guide arrives at the turning point. Often, the guide shows up after the decision to be courageous is made. But you can be confident that when you come to a turning point, a guide will always appear.

As you look back at your story, I'm certain you can think of some very specific voices who helped you in key moments in your story up to this point. It may have been something someone said in passing in a conversation that was the exact truth you needed in the moment. Maybe you discovered a book that spoke right to your situation. Maybe you met a mentor who helped you gain a whole new perspective. The person or book or sermon didn't tell you what to do, but they gave you insight and then left it to you to make the decision. Good guides simply point the way.

When you face a turning point and aren't sure what to do next, start paying attention, because you can be certain that a guide will show up. As the old Zen proverb says, "When the student is ready, the teacher will appear."

Follow Me, This Is the Way

Before I take a Summit Leaders team on a hike, I always do a scouting trip at the location way ahead of time. I've made that a personal rule. I don't want to be leading people somewhere I've never been. But one time, I broke my own rule, and the results were nearly disastrous.

I hiked almost all of the trail the team would be taking. But because of some inclement weather, I skipped one section of it. The section that I had hiked was pretty moderate. I figured the rest of the hike was the same. I looked at a topographical map, and the section I skipped wasn't too steep, so I assumed...

But you know what happens when you assume.

The part that I skipped was the hardest and most treacherous section of the trail. It was filled with giant boulders that you had to climb on all fours. Not only that, but the steepest sections of the trail were on solid granite that was extremely slippery, and it rained the night before our hike.

When the team asked me what the hike would be like, I shared what I knew—but I didn't know the entire trail. I had advertised the hike as moderate, but in truth, it was incredibly challenging.

Many team members weren't able to complete the hike because I hadn't prepared them correctly. I felt like a fool. But I learned an important lesson that day: If you really want to be prepared for a journey, you need to find a guide with firsthand, real-world experience of the entire trail—not just someone who looked at a map or read a book. You need someone who truly knows what's ahead and will guide you based on that knowledge.

Life is complicated. It's not always black-and-white, wrong-and-right decisions we face. Living with wisdom requires nuance and balance—which requires a lot of work. I know I would rather someone just give me a simple rule to follow. *Do this, don't do that.* I want a formula that'll ensure I'll be successful and get where I want to go. But…

There is no formula for life. There is only revelation.

Every year, we humans buy millions of books (thanks for buying this one, by the way) and attend conferences and webinars that promise a formula for success—in business, in relationships, in life. We want the "successful people" to share their secret to success. We want their formula. The problem is, there is no formula. Each person is unique. We all have different abilities, talents, experiences, and personalities. What worked for one person won't work the same way for you. You have to walk your own journey. Sure, you can benefit from other people's experience and use the principles they followed, but their formula will never work in your life exactly the way it worked in theirs.

We love formulas. We love checking boxes and expecting an outcome. *Do A, then B, then you'll get C.* Every time. It's certain and predictable. That's why humans have always been so drawn to religion. Religion is a clear formula. "Do this. Don't do that. And the Higher Power will be pleased with you. You'll have a ticket to Heaven." Religion keeps things simple—too simple.

We needed religion before Jesus showed up. It was a temporary solution to man's inability to approach God. Facing God is scary. Religion buffers us from having to seek direct communication with God by assigning a special priest or shaman or seer to hear from God and tell us the formula. Carl Jung was on to something when he talked about how one of the main functions of organized religion is to protect people against a direct experience of God.[1] We tend to want someone to talk to God for us and tell us what to do. It's easier that way.

I have a master's degree in counseling. People often think that means I offer advice. They'll say: "Tell me what I need to do." Should I marry? Or remarry? Should I spend the money? Should I change jobs? The weight of the decision and what it means for their life is so heavy that they want someone to take the responsibility off of them. When someone tells you what to do and it doesn't go well, you can blame the person who gave you advice. "They led me astray! It's their fault!" That's why we often prefer to just be told what to do. We can blindly obey.

But good counselors—good guides—give very little advice. The best counselors help you grow into your own ability to navigate complexity with wisdom. A big part of maturity, expanding the circle of who you are, is learning to take responsibility for your own decisions and their results. Someone who is constantly told exactly what to do will just become a robot who's helpless without someone giving them commands. They can also become very susceptible to being led astray or being controlled. God wants you to walk in strength, confidence, and freedom. You have a unique journey to walk, so that's why Jesus promised to send a Guide who will lead you.

Right before He left Earth, Jesus told His disciples, "I still have many things to say to you, but you cannot bear them now. When the Spirit of truth comes, he will guide you into all the truth."[2] Jesus essentially said: *You can't handle the truth! Not all at once, at least. It's too much for you.* Jesus was the fullness of truth in human form. We're still trying to figure out everything He taught. His teachings constantly reveal new truths to us throughout the seasons of our lives. I constantly find myself reading His words and getting a new understanding of what He was talking about. Truth is always unfolding to us.

Since Jesus knew we couldn't handle it all at once, He promised to send a Guide who would lead us in truth—the Holy Spirit. He is our guide in navigating the complexity of every circle and season of life. He gives revelation of the truth you need, in the amount you can handle, at the precise moment you need it along the journey.

There is no formula. There is only revelation from the Holy Spirit. Revelation is how we move past religion and walk in relationship with God. Religion—checking boxes and following a formula—isn't enough. Jesus said, "Unless your righteousness surpasses that of the Pharisees and the teachers of the law, you will certainly not enter the kingdom of heaven."[3] Religion is a start. It helps give you a framework for bringing your life into order, and we all need that order. But you have to move beyond just checking boxes. Only direct revelation can guide you through the complexities of the journey. Religion and formulas are small circles that don't expand you. Being led by the Spirit of God leads to revelation and growth.

The good news is, your Guide is always available. In fact, I believe He's been leading you even when you didn't realize it.

To the Roof of Africa

My friend Mike Navolio has taken over 120 people to the top of Mount Kilimanjaro (19,341 feet, or 5,895 meters)—the highest mountain in Africa and the highest free-standing mountain in the world. Climbing to the top of that beast is hard. Really hard! I've climbed it twice and made it to the top once. And I don't really have a lot of desire to put myself through that kind of pain and challenge on a regular basis. But Mike has done it over fourteen times. Oh, did I mention that Mike is seventy years old?! Did I also mention he did all this while working a full-time job? The guy is amazing. What's really mind-blowing is that he has raised millions of dollars to bring clean drinking water to villages in Africa through all those climbs. He actually climbs with a purpose.[4]

He recently retired from his job in the oil and gas industry so he could go full-time into taking teams to climb the mountain and repair broken wells in Africa. I asked Mike once how he got started with his mission. He told me, "Well, one thing led to another. Honestly, it all started with a selfish desire to go on a photo safari. I saw our church was doing a mission trip to Africa and they were going to do a safari at the end. So I went."

When Mike says "selfish desires," I always wince, because he talks about it like God turned his bad desires into good desires. But I'm convinced those desires were put there by God from the start.

One of my favorite verses is Psalm 37:4: "Delight yourself in the LORD, and he will give you the desires of your heart." When it comes to figuring out what you're called to do, one of the first places to look is at the desires of your heart—they're telling you something. Joseph Campbell often called it "following your bliss." God puts desires in your heart that, when you pursue them, will bring Him glory. And when you pursue them while seeking Him, they tend to lead you right to where you want to be.

Mike went to Africa on that mission trip and saw that teams would come from all over the world to dig water wells for villages, but the well would break soon after they left. Since the villagers had no resources to fix the wells, they went back to drinking bad water or walking miles to get it. Mike decided he would focus on raising money to repair broken wells and then bringing a team to do the work.

On a flight home from one of those trips, he struck up a conversation with a guy who had just climbed Mount Kilimanjaro and raised money for a project. People donated a certain amount for every foot of the mountain he climbed. Mike had always wanted to climb Kili—another desire God had put in him. And again, God used his desires to speak to him. Mike started doing annual trips to climb Kilimanjaro and raise money for the well projects. After the climb, team members went and repaired wells.

Since then, he has restored hundreds of wells all over Africa. The project is so successful and has raised so much money that he now employs four full-time men in Africa to repair wells year-round!

I asked Mike once, "At any point on this journey did you ever get a direct word from the Lord about what you were supposed to do? Did an angel appear?"

He laughed. "No way! It was all just a bunch of things lining up. One thing leading to another."

I've heard that line over and over and over from people who are doing amazing things: "One thing led to another." I'd be willing to bet that as you look at your life, you'd say the same thing about where you are today.

So, here's a crazy thought: What if one thing leading to another was actually the Holy Spirit guiding you?

God wants you to reach your destiny even more than you do. He created you for a work that He has prepared for you. He knows how to get you where you want to go. If you have a relationship with Jesus, He is leading you through the Holy Spirit, even when you don't know you're being led.

This is really, really good news if you're in a season where God seems silent right now. If you're looking to Heaven, trying to figure out what path to take but hearing nothing, I feel your frustration. I've been there many times. There's a verse that has been really comforting for me during those times. The prophet Isaiah talks about those seasons when you're facing adversity and looking for God, but He seems silent. He says, "And your ears shall hear a word behind you, saying, 'This is the way, walk in it,' when you turn to the right or when you turn to the left."[5] I take that to mean that we may only hear a word from our Guide if we're getting off track—to the right or left of the path. If you're on track, you probably won't hear anything. So keep moving ahead. If you aren't hearing from God, do the last thing He told you to do.

In a very real way—if you're seeking God's Kingdom to the best of your ability—if you aren't doing something wrong, then you're doing right. Even as I write that statement, the religious, formula-seeking side of me cringes. *Really? That seems like a dangerous way to think.* I've been conditioned to believe that I'm probably doing wrong most of the time. But that is condemnation, and there is no condemnation in Christ. It's a liberating and sobering thought to live by the words of Saint Augustine, who basically says, "Love God and do whatever you please: for the soul trained in love to God will do nothing to offend the One who is Beloved."[6]

If you get off track, you'll know it. The Guide will tell you.

God is always guiding us through the Holy Spirit. We just need to listen and pay attention. It's His responsibility to speak and ours to listen. Fortunately, our Guide has some very clear ways of communicating what we need for the adventure ahead.

The Voices of the Guide

Whenever I lead hikes around the world, I always have several local guides with us who are experts on the place. One guide takes the lead in front of the team. Another stays in the middle. Another comes behind the last hiker. Then I alternate between front and back. Essentially, on any given hike, we always have 3.5 guides (I'm the 0.5). When you've got 3.5 voices helping along the way, it's a whole lot easier for the team to get where they need to go.

I've seen the Holy Spirit, our Guide, consistently and reliably communicate using 3.5 specific sources of revelation:

1. **The Word:** The Apostle John called Jesus the *Logos*—the Word—that was with God from the beginning. Through His life and teaching, Jesus gave us the framework for how to live in harmony with the seen and unseen realities of life. The Bible records the entire story of God's revelation of truth, all leading up to Jesus.

The Bible is our unchanging map—an overview of how to live a life that pleases God.

The map never changes, but our understanding of the deep truths within it grows slowly. Like cutting through layers of an onion, the Bible has truth that continues to reveal itself in every circle and season of your life. The fact that you don't understand something in the map right now doesn't mean it's not relevant. It just means you may not be ready for that truth yet. But if you keep seeking truth, it will be given to you. Each layer of truth tends to be a bit painful and uncomfortable while it's doing its job. Like a fresh onion layer, the truth may burn our eyes a bit. But if you can surrender to that truth, it will set you free. And just when you think you are getting somewhere, the Guide will reveal more truth on the journey of life.

Big truth has to be revealed in layers.

This is how you can read the Bible your entire life and continue to gain new understanding. This also keeps us humble, realizing that we never know all the truth that can be known. The Bible is an inexhaustible source of truth. We see the truth through a hazy lens, at best.[7] In each circle, the Holy Spirit guides us into a deeper understanding of the truth we need for that season. You have the truth you need to walk out God's will right now. But there is always more truth to be learned.

Never discount any truth you find because it seems like only partial truth. In fact, all we ever have is partial truth. But that doesn't mean we should be discouraged. It means we stay humble, knowing there is always more to be revealed. We must constantly seek truth anywhere we can find it. If that truth lines up with the *logos*, then embrace it. The Holy Spirit will often use partial truth to lead us to greater truth. We have to stay open and teachable. If something makes you uncomfortable, there's a good chance there's a little truth in it that you need to embrace. Filter your experience on the journey through the Word and see what emerges. The Bible will always help you keep life in perspective.

In a hierarchy of guidance, the *logos*—God's Word—is at the top. But the Bible contains truth greater than any of us will fully understand—which is why God will often communicate His truth and guide us through people.

2. People: It's been said that the only thing that will change you are the books you read and the people you meet. God will often use people to help clarify direction and give insight in seasons of life. He'll also use books and teaching by people to help give insight you need on your journey.

God can speak through anyone. And often does. He even spoke through a donkey once. (The King James Version says it was an ass. Based on personal experience, I'd argue He still speaks through them today!) When we listen to speakers, writers, pastors, and teachers who speak truth that lines up with the Bible, it can point us to revelation. All truth is God's truth. Even flawed people can speak truth. (If you think about it, it's always flawed people who speak truth. There are only flawed people!) If we discount a message that contains truth because we don't like the messenger, we may miss out on important guidance we need for the journey.

God can give guidance through anyone, but more often than not, He uses the people who are deeply rooted in our lives—those who have earned the credibility to speak directly into our situation through their commitment to wanting the best for us. It's the people who know us best and love us most who are usually willing to tell us the things we don't want to hear. "Wounds from a friend can be trusted, but an enemy multiplies kisses."[8] You know you have a truly loving person in your life when they're willing to tell you uncomfortable truths they see about you and where you're heading. A good guide will tell you what you *need* to hear, not necessarily what you *want* to hear.

Giving those advisors authority to speak into your life can be a scary thing. I'm the type of person who wants to figure it out on my own. But the strange irony of God's freedom is that submission to authority gives us a layer of protection. When you have a guide who has lived more life than you and learned a few things, you'd be a fool to ignore their input.

Sometimes the best guidance is someone showing an example of what *not* to do. God can speak to us through anyone. He even uses those opposed to us, our enemies, to drive us to the exact place we need to be on our journey. Several years ago, a pastor I worked for really hurt me and created a major crisis. I look back now and see that I would not be doing what I am doing today—writing books and speaking—were it not for all the horrible stuff that happened with that pastor. God used that situation to guide me (even though it felt more like being pushed!) to the place I needed to be.

The Holy Spirit guides us through people. It may be through personal interactions or mentoring, or it may be through spending time reading a book written by someone who has the exact insight you need for this season. Over and over in my life, I've seen the Guide bring the exact book or teaching I needed into my life at the moment I needed it.

If you're feeling alone right now, look around; I'm certain the guidance you need is available. "If any of you lacks wisdom, let him ask God, who gives generously to all without reproach, and it will be given him."[9] If you'll humbly ask for help, the Guide will appear to help you in the exact way you need to hear it. When the student is ready, the teacher appears.

3. **The Inner Voice:** I've heard people from all philosophies and religions talk about listening to the inner voice. I think they're on to something. But know this, listening to the inner voice—following your heart—can be very dangerous. I've seen people who listened to their "inner voice" and ended up in serious trouble. They were sincere—sincerely wrong. The prophet Jeremiah talked about how our hearts are deceitful and can lead us astray. So just listening to your "heart" is a bad idea. We are masters at lying to ourselves.

But here's another one of those paradoxes of the faith: Our inner voice can lie to us, but God speaks through His Spirit within us. When you come into relationship with Christ, His Spirit actually comes and lives in you. How does that all work, exactly? I wish I could explain it, but that's way above my theological pay grade. It's a mystery. But the Apostle Paul explains it this way: "If the Spirit of him who raised Jesus from the dead dwells in you, he who raised Christ Jesus from the dead will also give life to your mortal bodies through his Spirit who dwells in you."[10] The Spirit of God within will actually speak to you. When God speaks to give guidance, it comes as a "gentle whisper."[11] So you'll have to quiet your mind and your own desires to hear it—but God promises He will speak.

My dad always used to tell me, "The first key to finding God's will is to have no will of your own." You know you've heard the inner voice of God when it doesn't contradict what the Bible says and, typically, it's confirmed by trusted advisors in your life.

3.5. Circumstances: I mention there are 3.5 ways God speaks, and this last one is the 0.5, because it should only be used to confirm what the first three are saying. God will often speak through circumstances, but circumstances alone aren't a good indicator of what action you should take. Sometimes circumstances line up well. Sometimes you have to move ahead in spite of circumstances that are far from ideal. Circumstances are a poor basis for making decisions, but often, they will confirm what we should do.

If you're seeking first the Kingdom of God, the Guide is leading you. Trust He's leading, even when He seems quiet or isn't giving as much clarity as you want. If you aren't hearing anything, do the last thing He told you. He'll make your next step clear. Then you'll need to be courageous and step into the unknown. But He'll be with you on the journey.

After prayer, listening, seeking counsel, and looking at the circumstances, it seemed like God was telling us to move to Mexico. I wasn't 100 percent certain, but there was enough confirmation that we concluded we needed to commit to moving forward.

So we did. Almost immediately, some amazing things began to happen. I got the signs I was looking for.

Which leads to the next stage in the circle—making the decision and committing to the path.

4

The Decision

Be bold, and mighty forces will come to your aid.

—Basil King

We felt more sure than unsure that we were supposed to move to Mexico, but there were still lots of hurdles we'd have to overcome. One of the huge challenges in front of us was raising monthly financial support from donors. I knew what this process was like because, as a kid, I had already walked a similar circle when our family spent endless Sundays going from church to church, sharing our vision for Guatemala, and asking folks to support us in our work down there. I knew what I was getting into, and I dreaded what it was going to take to raise all that money.

Typically, it takes about a year of traveling from church to church, talking to potential donors, and writing lots of letters to people to raise the support needed. So I immediately started announcing to our friends and family that we were planning to move to Mexico. I sent out a letter and asked them to consider supporting us. A major fear for me was how embarrassing it would be if we couldn't raise the money. I've known more than a few missionaries who felt very called to a place but, after facing the challenges of raising support, their call seemed to...disappear. It would be embarrassing, but part of me thought it would be a relief if we couldn't raise the money. At least we wouldn't have to go to Mexico. We could say we gave it a shot, but circumstances dictated otherwise.

The other concern was, typically, people don't start sending money until you're actually on the mission field—which is scary. You could end up going, but if people don't give, you get into a precarious financial situation.

I sent out the first letter, saying, "We feel called to Mexico, blah, blah, blah." I figured we'd get one or two responses to our plea for support. But what happened next blew my mind.

We received so many responses that we were fully funded after one letter! One. Letter.

God did a miracle. I felt partly excited, partly scared out of my mind. And partly irritated that I was actually going to have to do this! This was happening. I had asked for a sign—and I got it. But it only came after I decided to fully commit to the journey.

Oh, and then there was the icing on the cake: As if being fully funded wasn't enough, we also needed a truck to take with us. We had two trucks given to us!

Three months later, we moved to southern Mexico.

After the turning point, after summoning the courage to move forward while listening to the guide, there comes a point when you have to go all in. You have to decide to fully commit to moving ahead. Like Tarzan, swinging from vine to vine in the jungle, you'll have to let go of the one you're holding now and grab the new vine which hasn't been fully tested yet. If you decide to hold on to both vines, just to be safe, you'll be left dangling there, arms stretched between them, stuck.

You'll have to let go of what was and dive fully into the adventure of the new circle God is leading you into. The only way to move forward is to fully engage and be present with the journey ahead. You'll have to stop researching and analyzing and just live it out. Surrender the outcome and go all in. The good news is this: if you commit to the path, a way will open to you.

Committing to the Journey

There's a common theme in all the great stories we love: when an inciting incident happens, the hero has a moment of hesitation or reluctance about embracing the journey. They don't feel up to the task, or they realize how much total commitment will cost them. Even Jesus had a moment when He said, "Father, if You are willing, remove this cup from me. Nevertheless, not my will, but Yours, be done."[1]

When we start looking at what total commitment means, it's the most natural thing to be reluctant. Sure, the adventure promises some rewards, but we also know it's going to mean sacrifice. In the words of C. S. Lewis, "We are not necessarily doubting that God will do the best for us; we are wondering how painful the best will turn out to be."[2]

As we look at the journey ahead, we realize:

"If I commit to _____, that will mean _____." You can fill in your own blanks.

If I commit to really going all in on this marriage, that will mean I may get rejected and hurt.

If I commit to pursuing this call, I might fail and look foolish.

If I commit to being more generous, that will mean I won't have the safety net I might need.

If I commit to getting healthy, that will mean giving up some things I really love.

We know the price of going all in, which is why we tend to shrink back when the moment of truth arises. But there comes a point when not committing to the journey and your new reality actually ends up hurting you.

A friend of mine was diagnosed with diabetes. It was a major turning point in his life. A doctor explained to him all the changes he'd need to make in his lifestyle to manage his disease. But my friend didn't make the changes. It just seemed too overwhelming and felt like defeat to admit to it.

After several years of ongoing health struggles and multiple rebukes, the frustrated doctor made my friend read a sentence out loud that said: "I am a diabetic." My friend said that reading that line jolted him. He had been refusing to acknowledge his illness because of what it meant he'd need to change. But there was no way to manage (or potentially beat) his disease if he refused to commit to reality and this new journey. When he finally committed, he was able to start managing the illness and his quality of life vastly improved.

I think we all tend to respond the way my friend did, in one way or another. When we look at our new reality and what it means for us, it's pretty natural to just ignore the truth or numb ourselves. But even while we're ignoring it, it keeps making us miserable. We feel the push to be more than we are, and it just keeps pestering us if we don't commit. If we would just face the facts, get over our fear, and commit to the journey ahead, it could remove a lot of suffering.

Sometimes we try to hedge our bets. We try to keep one foot in the past and try to move forward at the same time. But it just doesn't work. Partial commitment to a new journey just creates confusion and anger. Can you imagine if you went into premarital counseling with your fiancé(e) and he or she asked the counselor, "Before we start, I just want to make sure I can still date other people after I'm married, right?" Major red flag! You'd know they weren't committed. The same is true for our journey. At some point, you have to go all in. You have to decide to embrace the adventure and be fully present in the season you're entering. Commit to giving all you have to the journey ahead. Don't look back, don't look too far ahead. Be present.

King Solomon warned: "Say not, 'Why were the former days better than these?' For it is not from wisdom that you ask this."[3] Looking back will just make you miserable and keep you from being present right now. Remember with fondness what used to be, but recognize that you can't go back.

But you also can't look too far ahead, which means choosing to not "worry about tomorrow, for tomorrow will worry about itself."[4] Focus your energy on this new adventure and determine that you will get every last drop of learning and training from it right now.

Think about your story so far. You'll see a handful of times when you fully committed, and it got you exactly where you are today. Chances are, you didn't really have a full understanding of what you were committing to. Who truly understands what getting married or having kids or getting healthy or fully committing to Christ will require? But you committed to what you knew, in faith. You fully committed to your spouse, and your marriage improved. You fully committed to getting healthy, and you feel stronger today. You moved to the new city, engaged with the people around you, and found a new community. You nearly backed out right before the big decision, but then you took the plunge and you survived. You had the grace for the challenge the moment you needed it.

The same will be true in this new season.

Of course, there may be a few incidents in your story when you took a risk and it failed miserably. God never promised that the result of your commitment would be exactly your desired outcome. But He promised that He'd complete the work He started in you. If you went all in and gave it your best shot, there's a good chance that what you perceived as failure will ultimately work for your good. Shelve your interpretation of that season and hold out for the long game; you never know what will come of it. But you can be sure it will be good.

So commit to what you know right now and trust God. Ask for a sign or two—that's fine. But don't hesitate too long. If you wait for 100 percent certainty, it will be too late. The ship will have sailed. I believe you'll get another chance, but you might end up wondering what could have been.

The path to your calling will rarely be perfectly clear at the start. But if you commit to the path, the way will open to you, one step at a time. And there's a good chance you'll begin to see wonderful things start to happen that are beyond anything you expected.

Forget Not All the (Unexpected) Benefits

The city where I live is right on the edge of the Texas hill country. This area is known for lots of cedar trees and oaks that tend to torture people with allergies. The year we moved here, I was in bed sick with allergies for weeks at a time from January to April. It was miserable. The allergies would turn into upper respiratory infections, and I was constantly having to visit the doctor.

About a year after our move here, right in the middle of the misery of allergy season, I really felt like I was supposed to start fasting on Fridays, like the early Christians did. Now, fasting one day per week may seem small to you, but I had never fasted an entire day in my life. Our youth group used to do these thirty-four-hour famine events where we stood in solidarity with the starving and raised money by not eating. I could never make it. I'd slip out and go to McDonald's while everyone else was involved in a group activity being spiritual. Yes, I was horrible—and weak.

I had tried multiday fasts before, but I'd get all hangry and un-Jesus-like, and that's not cool. So I figured fasting was just not for me. I'd commit to fast for two days and barely make it through one, which made me always wonder if that made me a halfast Christian. (Read that slowly now . . . and watch your language!) Anyway, I committed to fasting one day per week for spiritual reasons.

It was miserable.

I was grumpy and had a headache most of the day. But I would push through, just to prove to myself that I could do it. But then something completely unexpected happened. After a few weeks of fasting on Fridays, I found I started looking forward to it. My body started craving the break from eating, and I felt a lot more mental (and sometimes spiritual) clarity. Then I read somewhere that Christians used to fast on Wednesdays and Fridays. So I added another day to my fast every week and started to look forward to that, too.

After about nine months of fasting two days per week, I started to notice some subtle changes in my life. The most important thing was, during this season, God gave me some really clear direction about a step I needed to take that helped provide financially for my family and opened a door for ongoing ministry.

But there was more.

I noticed physical changes too. The extra weight around my belly that I had refused to admit was there (I told my wife it was muscle) went away. I lost twenty pounds without adding more exercise or even cutting back on what I loved to eat. Second, that next spring, my allergies didn't take me down sick! Third, I had a level of mental clarity I hadn't had in years. Fourth, I didn't get hangry anymore. I'd get hungry, but that hunger didn't control my mood or attitude.

On one of my hikes in Israel, I was telling a doctor about these small miracles. She explained that when my gut wasn't constantly processing food, it had time to fortify other areas of my body and burn off fat. She told me I would get the same health benefits if I started doing intermittent fasting three days per week. For three periods of twenty-four hours per week, I'd only eat during a six-hour window. I did it and loved the results. Now, I do it nearly every day! Fasting has completely changed my life—spiritually, mentally, emotionally, and physically.

Here's the thing, though. When I committed to fast, I had no idea I would get all those added benefits. I just set out to be obedient to the small step of fasting one day that I was supposed to pursue but didn't want to. I committed to the path and got loads of unexpected benefits.

And that's the nature of fully committing to the journey God places in front of you. You have no idea what lies on the other side of total commitment. There will be challenges. It will be hard and, at times, may feel unbearable. But know this: There will also be loads of unexpected benefits you can't even calculate into the equation right now because you just don't know what you don't know. You only get the benefits when you go all in.

When Jesus was on Earth, He invited all sorts of people to follow Him. One guy wanted to join the crew, but said, "Lord, let me first go and bury my father." Sounds like a reasonable request to me. Family is important after all. Right?

But Jesus said to him, "Leave the dead to bury their own dead. But as for you, go and proclaim the kingdom of God." Another guy said, "I will follow you, Lord, but let me first say farewell to those at my home." Jesus said to him, "No one who puts his hand to the plow and looks back is fit for the kingdom of God."[5]

Sweet, loving, compassionate Jesus didn't seem to have patience for a halfast commitment. I don't think He was trying to be harsh. I think His insistence on total commitment was actually loving. Jesus knew it's only when you fully commit that you get the benefits and rewards in the life of faith.

You only get abundant life when you go all in. It's a package deal. If you only partially commit, you'll just be miserable. Like a guy (basically) told me once, "Before I followed Jesus, I didn't feel guilty for taking advantage of people. Now I do. It was a lot easier when I was just living for myself." Some people have just enough of Jesus to be miserable. They feel horrible for not being what they know they should be but never lean into the power He offers to be all they could be. They keep holding onto their old life—habits, mindsets—and end up like Tarzan, dangling between two vines in no-man's land.

Total commitment to following Christ in every season will be hard. In the words of G. K. Chesterton, "The Christian ideal has not been tried and found wanting. It has been found difficult; and left untried."[6] Jesus asks hard, impossible things of us. But He also promises rewards and benefits. "Forget not all his benefits."[7] You get the benefits when you fully surrender your life and choose to be present in this season. When you fully commit to the path ahead, you can expect that God will open doors that are "exceeding abundantly above all that we ask or think."[8] You may find yourself doing things beyond your wildest dreams, living things you never could've even imagined you'd get to do.

Of Coffee and Crop Circles

I first met K. C. O'Keefe in a small cafe in the Andes Mountains of Peru. He was there to teach our team how to create an amazing coffee experience for a cafe we were about to start in Cuzco—right near Machu Picchu. I had no idea who he was when we first met. But after learning the ins and outs of coffee for an entire day, I soon found out that he is one of the top coffee experts in the world. He helps coffee producers across the globe to grow and harvest the highest quality coffee possible. Naturally, I wanted to know how he had become such an expert.

K. C. grew up in Seattle, Washington. After attending Bible school, he wanted to be a missionary teacher. He committed to doing whatever God placed in front of him. An opportunity opened to teach the Bible in a remote region of Peru, so he went. While he was there, he met a community of Christian coffee farmers and asked how he could help them. Because he was from the United States, they asked if he could help them get their coffee into the North American market. K. C. didn't know anything about coffee—he was a Bible teacher. But he was committed to serving the people however he could, so he started learning about coffee so he could help his fellow Christians.

That decision changed the course of his future.

He started studying all aspects of the coffee business. He worked on coffee farms. He started learning from coffee roasters and cafe owners. Putting one foot in front of the other, over the next several years, "one thing led another," and K. C. became one of the top coffee experts in the world. He now teaches coffee producers around the globe how to improve their crops and production for distribution. He has raised the average income for coffee farmers and farm workers in the regions in which he works. He has improved working conditions as well. What's fascinating to me about K. C. is that he never set out to be a coffee expert. He just had a vague call to be a missionary teacher. But when an opportunity presented itself to serve others, he went all in. He stepped out toward the call and, once he was in the right place, the path became clear to him. He *is* a missionary teacher—teaching about coffee all over the world. And he's having an impact he never could have dreamed possible.

If you connect the dots of K. C.'s story, you'll see some pretty clear circular patterns: He grew up in Seattle (a major hub for coffee) and had connections to the area. He wanted to be a teacher on the mission field. (And he is, just not the way he thought he would be.) To top it all off, a big part of what K. C. does involves building new equipment to help the production process in remote areas. He just designed and built a solar bean drier. He said he learned how to tinker and build things from his father, who was an engineer at Boeing. God was preparing K. C. before he even knew he was being prepared. When he committed to serve, wherever that path led, the way opened to him in a way he never could have foreseen.

I've seen this pattern over and over with people who are willing to fully commit to what God places in front of them. They think they're stepping out to do one thing, but once they get moving, they find out what the true call was. It's a law of physics and a law in God's order—a moving object keeps moving. It's way easier to redirect something, or someone, in motion.

Sometimes God just has to get you somewhere so you can find what you were really there to do. When He changes your direction, it often feels like a failure—like you missed His call. Sometimes we set out to do one thing and end up doing another. But that's fine. With the right perspective, you'll begin to see that what seemed like a false start or failure of your first effort was just the path God used to get you right where He wanted you.

Your story is no different than what K. C. experienced. The details will appear once you fully commit. The final destination might look different than what you expected, so stay open-minded and flexible. Remember, God wants you walking in your calling even more than you do. Trust that He's working out His plan in your life, even when you can't see the path ahead.

Commit to move forward, one step at a time. Let one experience build on another. Learn through each step. Sure, research and prepare—but in the wilds of the unknown, there will be things you can't prepare for. You have to trust that your Guide is leading you. Your willingness to fully commit will unlock the grace you need to face what's ahead. In the words of Basil King, "Be bold, and mighty forces will come to your aid."[9]

When to Take the Leap

When we committed to move to Mexico, we got the finances and the truck(s) we needed. And it happened way quicker than I expected. But first, we had to start moving ahead with the plan. We had to put ourselves out there and risk looking foolish if it didn't work out like we thought it would.

You'll have to do the same.

You won't get more clarity standing at the crossroads indefinitely. You only get clarity as you move forward. God will begin to show you the next steps, or He will make it really clear that you're on the wrong path. Trust me, He will make it clear. You'll know.

How will you know?

Well, first let me say this: facing challenges and opposition is not a sign you missed the boat (more on that in the next chapter). In fact, more often than not, opposition is a sign that you're on the right track. The obstacle is the way. That's why total commitment is so important. The road ahead will have some challenges, and you have to decide that you won't back out when you start facing resistance or pushback. But believe it or not, when you face opposition while you're pursuing the path God has for you, you'll find a peace deep inside.

Paul talks about the peace that transcends, or goes beyond, all understanding that guards your heart and mind.[10] When you're walking the path you're called to, there's peace—a quiet confidence—that shouldn't make sense based on what's happening around you. All around can be chaos and uncertainty, but you'll have a deep-seated calm inside that you're right where you need to be. That's how you'll know. Trust that peace.

If you don't have that peace and confidence—there's your sign.

It can be hard to sort out what's fear and what's lack of peace, so bring wise people around you in on the decision. If you've concluded it really is lack of peace, not just jitters that come with doing something new, then don't keep pushing ahead. Just turn around and try again. Take whatever steps are necessary to get to another path. There's grace if you misunderstand the call. And, honestly, very few decisions are irrevocable or unchangeable. Sure, there may be some embarrassment when you have to tell people plans changed or didn't work out (believe me, I know about this—more on that later), but most decisions aren't life-or-death if you get them wrong. So stop making it so epic and dramatic. Chill out a little, relax, and move ahead.

There are lots of ways to fully commit that don't require completely risking your life or your future. If you want to start a side hustle, it's wise to maintain your day job. But most experts will tell you that when you get to a point where you're making 50 percent of the income you need from your side hustle, then it's time to pull the plug on your stable job and take the leap. You'll never be able to achieve the next 50 percent you need to replace your current income until you go all in. You have to commit. Whether it's committing money, or time, or energy—there's a balance you can find between fully committing and being reckless.

One of the main reasons I resisted going to Mexico was because I was just starting my outdoor adventure organization. I was fully committed to making it happen, and I already had my first speaker—a prominent, nationally known leader—lined up to join me. I couldn't see how I could live in Mexico and do the outdoor adventure. But, looking back, I realize that taking the step of moving to Mexico is what ultimately led to starting the outdoor adventure organization on strong footing. I didn't see a way to balance it all. But once I committed, it all became clear. We have to make sure we don't get too hardheaded about how we think God needs to work. Stay flexible and move ahead with humility, trusting that God will guide you one step at a time. As my friend Marcus says, "As you go, you'll know."

I don't know many successful people who have ever gotten 100 percent certainty on risky decisions. (If they say they do, I think they're ignoring the facts!) You'll have to decide at what point you have enough confidence to move forward. For the record, when Emily and I feel about 60 percent certain that we're supposed to move forward, we do it. You'll have to figure out for yourself and those connected to you what your threshold will need to be. Just remember, you'll never get 100 percent certainty. In fact, if you get 80 percent, I'll be a little jealous!

Decide on a timeframe and a stop-loss plan. Step out and try it for a year. You can endure almost anything for a year. After that year, reevaluate. I tell people that when they commit to a reasonable timeframe, they shouldn't be evaluating on a daily or weekly basis how it's working out. There are too many ups and downs at first, and if you have a bad week or month or quarter, you'll be tempted to bail. Just move forward and reevaluate after setting a reasonable timeframe. If, after that time frame ends, it's clear this wasn't right, then stop. But I think you'll be surprised by what actually happens when you commit.

In fact, there's a good chance you'll start to ask yourself, "Why didn't I do this sooner?" Because you're right where you're supposed to be—venturing into the unknown on faith—you'll feel the sheer thrill of it all and might feel regret at having hesitated. But don't let that ruin things. Trust that God's timing is perfect. You weren't ready before. But you are now.

As you look back at your story, you'll see the pattern. You committed to the path, and the way opened to you. You decided to be present and engage with the path ahead. You didn't see any possible way things could work out, but you trusted God and took it one step at a time. And here you are today. What was true then is true now. If you fully commit to the path, a way will open to you.

So, let me ask a question: What will fully committing look like for you in this season? In your personal life? In your health? In your marriage? In your spiritual journey? What will it take to go all in and be present right now?

Do you need to:

Sign the papers and surrender the outcome?

Let go of what will never be and embrace what actually is?

Clean out your pantry and fridge of anything that will tempt you?

Get rid of that substance you have stashed away that you go back to over and over again when life gets stressful?

Delete the number of the person who is your backup plan if your marriage doesn't improve?

Get off social media completely?

Make the call or write the email?

What will be the grand gesture that shows you're going all in for this season? May I suggest you do it. Posthaste.

Yes, it will be scary. After you commit, you'll probably question your decision and doubt yourself. Your commitment will probably require sacrificing something you value greatly—time, money, energy, a dream.

But . . . you have no idea what is waiting on the other side of your decision to fully commit to the path in front of you.

It will be full of amazing surprises. Some good, some difficult. If you've fully committed, you'll be armed with the strength and resolve that will get you through what lies ahead. And in that process, you'll get even stronger, because it's the challenges and struggles in every circle that develop strength, character, and the skills you'll need to share your message and find meaning and purpose in your story.

Struggles make you stronger. Which is what we'll talk about next.

The Adventure
(aka The Challenges)

Opportunities to find deeper powers within ourselves
come when life seems most challenging.
—Joseph Campbell

From the moment we arrived at the property in Mexico, I knew my work was cut out for me. David and Karen had been gone for several months by the time we got there, so little to no maintenance had been done on the property. The retreat center portion of the ministry was right on the beach, so the salty air had quickly rotted pretty much everything. There was a green, slimy swamp in the back that had previously been a pool. Several pumps and water heaters were no longer working. Appliances were broken and rusted out. Tropical vines had grown into the plumbing. Seemingly endless maintenance needed to be done, and I had never repaired anything in my life. I figured I'd have to hire people to get things back into order.

I called David to ask who I should call to repair some of the problems. He laughed and told me no one would come out there—

I'd have to fix things. Talk about frustration and anger. I wasn't a repairman. I was there to do "ministry." But I was about to get a whole new perspective on what ministry can look like.

Once I faced the fact that no one was coming to rescue me, I reluctantly set out to attack all the projects. I had to learn to repair, well, pretty much everything—gas water heaters, air conditioners, roof tiles broken by falling coconuts, and pool pumps with all sorts of bizarre things caught in them.

And there was the water situation. Our property only got water from the city about once per week, so we had a giant cistern that held our weekly water supply. One day, the pump in that cistern broke, and of course, it was on the one day that we had gotten water from the city. The cistern was completely full. So I had to dive down through a tiny hole in the ground into the deep tank and fix the pump issues while holding my breath.

That was just the maintenance portion. I also quickly realized just how unsafe the area was when we left town one weekend and someone broke in and stole all our church's sound equipment, lots of electronics from our house, and all sorts of tools. I was furious. The worst part was, I knew people in the neighborhood knew who had stolen it all. Everyone knew everything that went down there. So I started asking around. People would look down at the ground. "*No sé.*" ("I don't know.") Everyone was protecting the guilty party.

After some aggressive investigating, someone showed up at our house and said, "I think I know who took your stuff."

He led me down to a small shanty in an alley. A young man was sitting on one of the speakers stolen from the church, wearing a haughty grin. "I saved your stuff from the *ladrones* (thieves)," he said.

I played along. "Really? Who stole all this?"

"A group of people from the mountains. I stopped them."

Likely story. "Oh yeah? All by yourself?"

"Yes. I'm a hero." He smirked.

"What did they look like?" I could feel heat rushing to my cheeks and forehead.

He shrugged. "There are lots of faces in the world, man. It's hard to remember."

I had no desire to keep playing this game. So I went on the offense. "I think you did it." I started ranting about what kind of a lowlife he must be to steal from a church. The conversation got heated. The guy who had brought me to the shack was really nervous. After an aggressive verbal exchange, the "hero" agreed to bring all my stuff back, for a small fee. I paid him and stormed out.

On the walk back home, the guy who had brought me started rebuking me. "That guy is dangerous. You shouldn't have talked to him that way."

After my anger calmed down, I started to realize how foolish I had been, dealing with him like that. But I was fed up. I felt like I was constantly dealing with corruption. Everywhere I turned was a battle of some sort. Everywhere.

When it came to harassment and corruption, nobody was better at it than the local cops. As soon as they saw my face or the Texas license plate on my truck, they would pull me over and hit me up for a bribe. I never paid. I came to detest the corrupt police. All around us, drug lords were involved in open shootouts in public places and people were dying, but the cops were pulling me over for not using a blinker (nobody uses their blinker there!) and harassing me for a few bucks.

One day I was driving through town, doing absolutely nothing wrong, and a cop who was driving the other direction saw me. His face lit up and he turned on his lights, motioning to me. I made a snap decision. He was in a tiny four-cylinder car. I had a much bigger engine. Plus, he was still in the process of turning around to come after me. I knew I could outrun him. So I slammed my foot on the accelerator and made a run for a mountain tunnel that leads out of town. I hit a hundred miles per hour in that tunnel. Talk about total commitment! The young man in the car with me was freaking out, looking out the back window. I actually managed to outrun the corrupt cops. (I won't be writing any books on how to be a docile, culturally sensitive missionary any time soon.)

Life in Mexico was a constant battle. From paying a light bill to getting groceries, nothing was easy. It felt like one obstacle after another. One challenge after another.

You don't have to move to another country or face corrupt cops to figure out pretty quickly that life is filled with challenges and struggles. I know you've had your own seasons of constant battles. We all face them in this life. In fact, that's one of the few things that all the great philosophies and religions of the world agree on—life is difficult.

For whatever reason, God has chosen to use those very struggles as the means to making us into who He intends us to be. Difficulty has a way of revealing parts of us we didn't even know were there. Challenges pull potential out of us.

That's why, in every great story, adventurers face a series of struggles that stretch them and cause them to grow. The hero sets out on a journey to climb a mountain, discover truth, save the world from destruction, face off with dark forces, and overcome their own mental or emotional hurdles. The more conflict and tension in a story, the more engaged we are. We keep watching the movie or reading the book, cheering for the hero, because we want to see him or her defy impossible odds. We read books and watch movies because we love the struggle and challenges.

Other peoples' challenges, that is.

But when it comes to our challenges, well, that's another story. If you're like me, when life gets hard, I start asking, "Why me? Did I do something wrong?" Like I expect life to be easy and some unique burden has been placed on me. But the simple fact is we all face challenges and struggles, and those difficulties make us grow. They stretch and push us to become more than we are right now. Which is why God uses specific struggles and challenges in every season to build us into who we are made to be.

We Need Conflict

John was born right on his due date, a prophetic sign of what would define his life. His birth happened at a very convenient time: 12:33 p.m.—just in time for the obstetrician to get to his favorite restaurant before the lunch specials ended. He was born healthy and strong, no complications.

When John was nine months old, he started walking. He was talking by age two. When he was four, he started kindergarten. He did well. In fact, he did great through all of elementary and middle school. Everyone got along with him. He excelled in sports and had great grades.

When John was seventeen, he got early acceptance into four different top-ranked schools. He graduated from college with a 4.0

GPA. Right out of college, he got a job with a Fortune 500 company. His first day at work, he met Gina. They fell in love and were married nine months later. Gina's family loved John, and he loved them. John's family loved Gina, and she loved them, too. Christmases and holidays were filled with peace and joy, and everyone got along perfectly.

John and Gina had three children. Each of those children was born on their exact due dates, at the most convenient times. They were all healthy. The kids brought John and Gina even closer together, and they became more and more connected in their relationship...

Okay, I have to stop now. I can't handle it anymore.

Would you agree with me that, so far, this is the most boring story you've ever read? It's pleasant, but I'm guessing the entire time you were thinking the next paragraph was when things were going to get bad. Something had to go wrong. It was all too perfect.

When we read a story, we expect that something is going to go wrong. We read or watch stories because of the conflict. We want to watch the hero overcome challenges. We want the hero to emerge victorious. Conflict is part of the adventure. We want conflict in a story so badly that professional storywriters recommend the inciting incident in a movie or book—the conflict the character has to face—happen as quickly as possible. Get the viewer or reader immediately engaged with conflict, then you'll keep their attention. A little setup, then straight into the conflict and challenges.

In every great story, it's the conflict that makes the main character a better person. He or she faces a journey fraught with peril and danger and struggles—traipsing through Middle Earth, venturing out into new star systems in the galaxy, or exploring the

Land of Oz. The character grows through tests and trials in the unknown.

Something deep inside us knows that the struggle is part of the journey. Heroes are made by hard times. We're drawn to this truth because it's part of the pattern of how God works. God didn't even let His own Son off the hook when it came to trials and tribulations that built Him. There's a strange verse in Hebrews 5:8 that says Jesus actually learned obedience through His suffering. Why would Jesus need to learn anything? I'll leave that to the theologians to debate, but here's the truth: Challenges are what pull out our potential. We're actually hardwired to grow stronger through our struggles. Everyone who becomes all they can be gets there by facing difficulty and resistance.

The Battles That Build You

My wife Emily is way tougher than me and isn't one to complain. But for as long as I've known her, she has struggled with stomach issues. She's also had ongoing headaches for as long as we've been married. (There's no connection between the headaches and living with me—really.) It has been a source of constant frustration for her. We visited doctors, got scans, and took different medications trying to resolve it. But nothing the doctors offered seemed to work.

So over the years, through trial and error, she went on a quest to solve her health issues. She read and studied. She learned what she can and can't eat. She's had to remove gluten, dairy, peppers and tomatoes (all nightshades), soy, and loads of other random things from her diet. Basically, she can only eat air and drink water.

Just kidding, sort of. Thanks to those changes, Emily is stronger and healthier now than she has been since her teens. But it's been quite an emotional struggle for her because she really enjoys food.

She was talking to me about the frustration of all the sacrifices she's had to make just to stay healthy. She sees what other people can eat and it just doesn't seem fair. She told me once, "I feel like my body betrayed me." There was a lot of emotion in that statement. I really feel for her. It really isn't fair.

I don't know why some people face greater challenges than others—health challenges, relational challenges, spiritual battles. There are lots of variables—geography, genetics, just bad timing. It really isn't fair that some people can eat whatever they want and seemingly get away with it. It isn't fair that some seem to have perfect health with no effort, while others struggle just to function normally. It's not fair that some people seem to float through life with doors of opportunity just flying open for them. It's not fair that some people had a better upbringing, got a better education, have more connections, or don't have all the anxiety and worry you and I carry.

We all have a unique burden to bear. And no, it's not fair. The thing is, there are some things that just are what they are. We can sit around moaning and complaining about our unique challenges—our body type, where we live, the stage of life we're in—and just be miserable. Or we can embrace our unique struggle and trust that somewhere in there, God is working something for His purposes. Your unique struggles are preparing you for a unique work.

On my wife's journey to getting healthy, she has gained a crazy amount of knowledge about health and wellness that healed her headaches and digestion issues. Much of it is outside the conventions of medical science and drugs. It uses food to heal. (Imagine that, God actually gave us natural ways to heal our illnesses! Excuse my sarcasm, please.) Emily regularly finds herself encouraging people who are having all sorts of autoimmune health issues that doctors can't quite diagnose or have just given medication to help the person manage. Emily shares her story and some things that have worked for her, and in the process, she's been able to point many of them in a direction to getting healthy.

Her struggle has been nearly unbearable for her at times. But she's beginning to see how that struggle is something that prepared her to help others.

Your story is no different. It's not fair that you have the burden you're forced to carry. But its highly likely that your greatest struggle is strengthening you so you can strengthen others. Every circle and season comes with unique challenges. Those struggles are the training ground for what's ahead. The good news is, God will be there with His grace to walk with you through those times. And as you press on ahead, you'll find yourself getting stronger.

What Doesn't Kill You Makes You Stronger

After we left Mexico, Emily and I moved to Cuzco, Peru, to start a cafe (I'll tell you more about that later). Cuzco sits eleven thousand feet above sea level high in the Andes mountains of South America. The altitude is really hard on your body and immune system because you're getting less oxygen. We had been living at sea level in Mexico, so for the first several months in Peru, I was constantly getting sick with lots of upper respiratory issues like bronchitis.

Someone (subtly) told me that if I'd start getting into shape, my body would be able to better fight off the challenges that come with altitude. So reluctantly, I started lifting weights and jogging. The altitude made it way harder than I had expected, but I committed and pushed ahead.

Two things quickly happened.

First, I stopped getting sick. Second, for most of my life I had been a skinny guy. I didn't like that but could never seem to put on any weight. But as I worked out and had to eat more to keep myself nourished, I started getting thicker and less skinny. The harder I pushed, the healthier and stronger I got. You'd think the best thing for feeling weak, tired, and sick from lack of oxygen would be to rest and take it easy—which is necessary at times—but as I researched, I learned that your body is made to be pushed and shocked up to a certain point. We need some stress to grow stronger. Doctors and psychologists call it eustress, or good stress. A healthy amount of stress and resistance actually makes you stronger and more resilient.

The economist and philosopher Nassim Nicholas Taleb says there are three types of organisms in the world—fragile, robust, and antifragile.[1]

Fragile systems break and crumble when they're exposed to stress, pressure, or disorder. A piece of fine china is fragile. If it breaks, it is irreparably shattered.

Robust organisms are unaffected when they face disorder or stress; they don't change. A boulder is robust. You can kick it and throw things at it, but it won't be affected.

You'd think fragile and robust are opposites, but they aren't. Fragile systems are broken by stress. So the opposite of fragile is something that would get stronger with stress. There's another kind of organism, something Taleb calls "antifragile." Antifragile organisms get stronger when confronted with shocks to their system. Chaos, disorder, and stress—followed by some time for recovery—make antifragile systems even stronger and more powerful.

You are antifragile. God made you that way.

You aren't invincible. But a certain level of stress and struggle is actually good for you. When you face emotional and physical struggles and are given proper time to recover, you get stronger. Physical, emotional, and spiritual strength all come through resistance and struggle. I wish the path to strength was filled with eating chocolate cheesecake and thinking happy thoughts, but it's not. I don't know exactly why God works this way, but for whatever reason, "We must go through many hardships to enter the kingdom of God."[2] Hardship and resistance are the path to strength.

If you've ever tried to build muscle through exercise, you've learned that no pain means no gain. To build muscle, you actually have to tear the fibers a bit. When you are in pain after a workout, you don't wonder what's wrong with you. No, you know pain is part of the process. Even though it's uncomfortable, you have a sense of satisfaction that you're getting stronger.

When those torn muscles are given proper time to recover, they heal back stronger—which is why professionals tell you to leave recovery days of no exertion in your schedule. It's the same thing that happens when you break a bone. The bone heals back stronger if it's set correctly and given time to recover. God made us to grow stronger through conflict and resistance—physically, emotionally, and spiritually. It's part of the process of making us who we're called to be. Life doesn't get easier; we get stronger.

The crazy thing is, if you treat an antifragile system like it's fragile, it actually becomes fragile! When antifragile systems are babied or overprotected, you do them a disservice. They become weak and prone to being hurt by minimal stressors. When life is too easy, we get weak and become vulnerable to being taken out by small struggles.

Everything God asks us to do makes us stronger. Every command He gave was for our benefit and strength. We've all felt weak and compromised when we violate our conscience, lie or deceive, or don't do what we know we should do. But there's a strength and confidence that comes when you know you're doing what's right. Walking in line with what God asks makes us bold. "The righteous are as bold as a lion."[3]

Again, we come to another paradox of the faith.

Strength is God's goal for us. But the kind of strength He wants for us requires a perspective shift. In His Kingdom, what feels like weakness can lead to ultimate strength—because the kind of strength God wants for us is strength on a spiritual level. In exercise, we say that if you want to really build muscle, you have to lift a particular weight until failure—until your body can't do it again. What's true in weightlifting is true in all of life. Failure is actually a path to growth, if you allow it to be. If you never fail, it means you aren't trying anything difficult. Which means you're probably playing it safe and going with what you know. If you really want to excel, you must risk the glorious. You must push yourself beyond what you think you can do. You have to try to do hard things that might result in failure. Even when you fail, you're growing stronger. In a very real way, what doesn't kill you makes you stronger.

In the struggles of life, God will often push us beyond what we think we can handle. He does this so we're forced to lean on His strength rather than our own ability. That's what the Apostle Paul heard from God in his own personal struggle: "My grace is sufficient for you, for my power is made perfect in weakness."[4] Strength is the ultimate goal, but the path to strength often feels like defeat, weakness, and failure at first. Feeling weak isn't a bad thing if it leads you to the source of ultimate strength—the love of God.

That's why James said, "Count it all joy, my brothers, when you meet trials of various kinds, for you know that the testing of your faith produces steadfastness. And let steadfastness have its full effect, that you may be perfect and complete, lacking in nothing."[5] The challenges in every season prepare and perfect us for the next level. They push us beyond our own strength and drive us to the power of God's love as our source—which is what real spiritual strength looks like. Challenges and struggles are the gift God gives us to help us reach our potential.

There are two particular challenges that I've found are jet fuel for launching us to our highest calling: enemies and limitations.

The Gift of Your Enemies

If Joseph wasn't sure how much his brothers hated him, being sold as a slave in cross-border human trafficking probably made it clear. Joseph had enemies. Sadly, they were his own family. In spite of being victimized by them, he kept a good attitude and served his master in Egypt well. But then, after resisting the sexual advances of his master's wife, he was falsely accused of a crime and thrown into prison. It went from bad to worse. In prison, he was forgotten by the guy who might have been able to bail him out. If I were Joseph, at this point, I doubt I'd have the mental and emotional fortitude not to give into despair and anger. Joseph was doing right, but his enemies always seemed to prevail.

Even when we're doing right, we will always have people who oppose us. Jesus was perfect, but people opposed Him. In spite of that, He said, "Love your enemies and pray for those who persecute you."[6] That statement seems absurd (and impossible) until you realize that your enemies are often the tool God uses to push you to your destiny. If God is really working all things together for your good, then *all things* include: the illness that is attacking your body, the person trying to get you fired so they can get your position, and the people who are attacking you because of your convictions. They're responsible for their actions, but their actions aren't stronger than God's ability to redeem what they do and bring something glorious from it. Moreover, if you can keep your perspective lifted, there's a good chance you'll become the force God uses to rescue the very people who were your enemies.

In one glorious day, Joseph got promoted to the second most powerful position in Egypt. The betrayal, slavery, and prison had prepared him for his greatest moment. Not only was he prepared to manage the kingdom, he was prepared to use his strength to help the people who had been his sworn enemies—his own family. When his family came begging for help so they wouldn't starve, he managed to connect the dots and saw the big picture. He told them, "You intended to harm me, but God intended it for good to accomplish what is now being done, the saving of many lives. So then, don't be afraid. I will provide for you and your children."[7]

God can turn your enemies into your mission if you'll keep your perspective lifted in the fray. You will often be called upon to lead the very people who hurt you away from their own destruction. This is what a true hero looks like. Just like Joseph, Jesus lived that example, and calls us to do the same.

The Gift of Limitation

When we discovered all the things my wife couldn't eat, I had to start paying closer attention to ingredients I was using. I love cooking creative things, but I remember thinking, *Man, this is gonna be impossible!* Everything I loved to cook had all the foods that were trying to kill her! I had to get creative and learn all sorts of alternate ingredients—tamari, tiger nut flour, coconut oil—things I didn't even know existed. Within a very short amount of time, I didn't feel any sense of limitation when it came to cooking. In fact, I don't even think about it much anymore. I know what I can cook and what I can't. I know what I can substitute for certain ingredients that I can't use. I know the boundaries, and I'm free to create within those boundaries.

T. S. Eliot once said, "When forced to work within a strict framework, the imagination is taxed to its utmost—and will produce its richest ideas. Given total freedom, the work is likely to sprawl."[8] He's talking about writing, but I think that quote applies across the board. In a world full of seemingly endless possibilities, limits are a gift. When we're limited, we know what we have to work with and are stretched to get creative within those limits.

Having too many options tends to hinder us. Barry Schwartz wrote an entire book, *The Paradox of Choice*, filled with studies about how too many options and unlimited freedom can actually have an overwhelming effect that paralyzes us. You've probably been to a restaurant that has so many items on the menu that you can't even choose what you want. You just end up going with what your friend ordered to make it simple. Limits keep things simple.

Limitation also breeds creativity. We're made in our Creator's image, so I believe all of us have creative capacity. But those capacities probably won't come out until you're under some pressure to be creative. If you're struggling to be creative or feeling bored with life, maybe it's time to commit to a path and limit your options. Say no to other possibilities and pick one—then figure out how to thrive in that limitation.

You'll Have It When You Need It

Now, if you're like me, the truth that challenges and struggle are an inevitable part of every season of life isn't exactly comforting. I'm just not to the point where I can say I rejoice in suffering. In fact, most of my biggest worries and fears are related to how to *avoid* future suffering. When things are going fairly well, I've ruined many a peaceful night wondering when it's going to get bad again. *Just how bad is it going to get?*

Jesus knew our tendency to worry about the struggles ahead, which is why He said, "Do not worry about tomorrow, for tomorrow will worry about itself. Each day has enough trouble of its own."[9] Jesus asks us to live in day-tight compartments. I believe this is a key to getting through the adventure-and-challenge stage of each season.

Stay focused on today. Be present today. Commit to learn what the struggle has to teach you today.

When the Israelites were doing their circle season in the wilderness, slowly making their way to their destiny while God toughened them up and strengthened them for what was ahead, He gave them just enough food from Heaven for that day. If they stored up more, it was rotten by the next morning. I think the lesson here is this: You will have the grace you need when you need it. But not before. So focus on today.

Paul said, "Endure hardship as discipline."[10] You've been wanting to be more disciplined, right? Here's your chance. Discipline your mind to stay focused and engaged on what's right in front of you. Do whatever it takes to keep your perspective lifted in the battle today. When tomorrow comes, you'll have the grace you need for its challenges.

When I look back at all the challenges we faced in Mexico, I wouldn't wish that experience on anyone. And I definitely don't want to do it again. I have some regrets about how I didn't keep things in perspective. I got so frazzled and irritated. But the further I get down the road, looking back, I see just how important that season was in preparing me for the future. I learned new skills. I also saw some dark sides of me that I needed to deal with.

When life gets hard in the circle you're in, you'll have to decide how you choose to see those struggles. Will you complain and cower to the challenges? Or will you stand up straight, put your shoulders back, and see the challenges for what they are: strength training and preparation for glory?

If you can get a new perspective on your struggles and begin to see them as part of the upward circle that is pushing you to your destiny, making you stronger, it can help shift how you see your current situation. Remember, you've been through battles before and God helped you through. He'll do it again this time.

Embrace the struggle in the adventure. Don't create unnecessary suffering or make life harder than it needs to be. But don't run from necessary suffering—the kind that makes you stronger. Trust that when God says, "My grace is sufficient for you, for my power is made perfect in weakness,"[11] He means it. It'll be there when you need it. Challenges will come, but right in the middle of it, you can be confident that "this light momentary affliction is preparing for us an eternal weight of glory beyond all comparison."[12]

What man actually needs is not a tensionless state but rather the striving and struggling for a worthwhile goal.

—Viktor Frankl

The Dark Cave

Faith is a dark night for man,
but in this very way it gives him light.

—John of the Cross

I knew we were in serious danger when one of our church members came to our house and, very secretively, offered me his pistol. "Joël, word on the street is that they're going to try to get revenge on you tonight. I think you should take my gun."

Guns are illegal in Mexico (like get-you-thrown-in-prison-for-life illegal), so I was more than a little concerned. "How do you have a gun?" I asked.

He looked down at the ground. "It's better you don't ask. But I know what these guys are capable of. Take the gun to protect your family."

I refused the weapon, but I could feel the anxiety building in me. *What were they going to try?*

The tensions that led to this standoff with one of the most dangerous guys in the neighborhood started when, against my better judgement, we *sort of* accepted an intern from the United States to come work with us. I say sort of, because it all got kind of pushed on us. I never actually got to talk to her before she came down. I only talked to her pastor and father who both said she was really looking forward to doing "mission work." They also mentioned in passing that they thought it would help "get her back on the right track." That line should have been a warning to me, but I felt so overwhelmed by everything happening to us that I wanted someone there to help us. Plus, misery enjoys company. So I sort of said yes.

Little did I know how much trouble that intern was going to create for us.

The first week she was there, I noticed an immediate surge in attendance at our Bible studies. I thought it was because word was getting out in the barrio that I was a great teacher. When I called David to tell him the good news about our growing attendance, he laughed. "Is it all guys showing up?"

My mind flashed back to the most recent meeting. "Uh…yeah."

"It's because of the new girl, your intern."

His bluntness kind of irritated me. But I soon came to realize he was right. The worst part was, she struck up a "connection" with a very volatile and dangerous dude—a guy who had shot someone a few years earlier and fled from the law but was somehow back in town. Our sweet, lovable little intern started sneaking out of the house to "evangelize" him. I knew we needed to send her back home.

We called her dad and decided it would be best to tell her right before her flight, to avoid her trying anything. The morning we broke the news, major drama ensued that I don't have the word count to explain here—but after the chloroform took effect, we managed to load her up and took her to the airport. (Of course, I'm kidding about the chloroform . . . or am I?) Putting her on a plane home felt like such a relief.

But the drama had just begun back in our barrio.

The guy she had fallen for was not happy. As soon as we got home, he started pounding on our front gate, yelling threats. People in the barrio started coming over and telling us, "He's gonna do something to get you back."

That's when we were offered the gun, and I started to realize just how volatile things were.

I called David. He wasn't comforting. He said, "Yeah. He's gonna do something. He has to save face. But who knows what? Just be vigilant."

We were holed up in our house for days. I just knew something terrible was going to happen to us. I considered sneaking out and flying back to the U.S. until things calmed down. I had dealt with anxiety before, but this was a whole new level. For the first time, I felt the potential of my life being threatened. I was scared and prayed a ton.

One particular night, we heard several threats and had a feeling something bad was going to go down. That same day, I got an email from a missionary friend in Africa who said she woke up in the middle of the night and felt like she really needed to pray hard for us. You know it's bad when God wakes up a missionary in deepest, darkest Africa to pray for you!

That night, when it seemed like things were going to go down, it rained all night. I felt like God sent that rain to protect us. I also found out later that the guy who offered me the gun had spent the evening patrolling our property to protect us. It was a dark and scary few weeks, filled with lots of fear, anger, and anxiety.

Eventually, we resolved things with the guy who was angry at us and got back to work. Our ministry seemed back on track.

But then, because of some complicated politics within the organization that owned the property where we were working, the decision was made by the board of leaders in the United States that it was time to close the ministry. A few short weeks later, David and Karen came down to help give pretty much everything away to local ministers and friends, then we packed up our vehicle caravan and began driving north toward the United States border together.

I remember alternating between about seventeen different feelings, sometimes all within one minute. I felt relief that all the challenges we had faced in Mexico were now behind us. Embarrassment about trying to explain why we had gone to Mexico in the first place. *What was the point of all that? What a waste of time and energy.* I felt like a failure. Deep down, I knew the ministry needed to end, but I couldn't help but feel guilty that it happened on my watch. (People don't usually like seeing that you closed or ended things on a resume.) That feeling led to anger about the whole experience. It seemed to have no meaning or purpose. It was like we had just wasted a whole good year of our young lives. There were no success stories or radical conversions. In many ways, it seemed we had left the neighborhood in Acapulco worse than we found it. We hadn't changed our environment; it had changed us.

I had followed God, best I knew how, and it seemed like He led me to failure. He had walked me off a cliff and right into one of the biggest struggles of my life up to that point. There was no happy ending to it all. It just felt messy and unresolved. I was more than a little angry at God. I didn't want to pray. I didn't want to read my Bible. I didn't want to talk about it. I just wanted to get on with life.

I know you've had moments like that too. A time of confusion and disappointment with God. A season where it feels like your faith is floundering. You really thought God was going to save your marriage, but He didn't. You believed He'd provide, but He didn't. You were certain He would rescue the business, but He didn't. You thought He'd heal your child, but He didn't. You thought He'd protect you, but He didn't. When the ways you feel God let you down start stacking up, it's only natural to get frustrated and disappointed. We feel like the snail I mentioned at the start of the book that was thrown across the yard through no fault of his own. *What was that all about?*

When you hit this stage of the circle, know this: You didn't mess up. It's part of the process. With each circle in our story, the challenges and struggles we face ultimately lead us to a low, dark point. A moment when all hope seems lost. We come to a decisive battle when we face off with darkness and doubt within us and around us. The hero enters a cave and confronts an enemy. Luke Skywalker confronted Darth Vader. Frodo faced off with his own desires to keep the ring rather than toss it into Mount Doom. Dorothy faced off with the Wicked Witch of the West. Sometimes it's a confrontation with something outside of you. But more often, it's an internal battle with your own thoughts and emotions.

When the hero fights that ultimate battle, he emerges transformed. On the other side of that dark cave is a new perspective and a whole new world. But to get to the new world, you have to stumble through the darkness and face off with the enemy for a while.

So let's talk about what to do when you find yourself in that dark cave.

The Dark Night of the Soul

While writing this book, the area where I live got hit with the worst winter storm in over one hundred years. We had single-digit temperatures and loads of snow and ice that took out our state's power grid, leaving millions without heat for days. On the second day without power, when it got down to forty degrees in my house, I pulled out my flashlight and started digging deep into a dark storage closet for more warm clothes. I found all sorts of amazing winter gear I'd completely forgotten I had because I never need it in Texas.

Sitting there in the glow of that flashlight, I started thinking about the last few years. If I'm honest, I've felt forgotten in God's closet for a while. I've been patiently waiting for Him to use me in a big way, but in the meantime, time is ticking away and I'm not getting any younger here. I kind of wonder if one day He'll flip the light on, look in the closet, and go, "Oh, hey, Joël! You're still in here? Sorry, bro. I forgot about you!" I think we've all felt like those forgotten clothes in the closet from time to time. We all wonder if God set us aside for a season and then completely forgot we were there. *Do you see me down here, God?*

I tend to agree with Father Ron Rolheiser when he says that one of our greatest fears is being forgotten in God's closet. If I'm honest, I have to admit that over the last few years, God has seemed pretty silent—at least on the things I want Him to communicate with me about. During His silence, I've questioned a lot of things I believed about Him. *Does He really have a plan? Did I miss His will somehow?*

I don't doubt God loves me. I don't doubt His goodness. I'm grateful for all He's done in my life. I even know He made me for a purpose. For the most part, life is actually quite good. I can't complain. I've done my best to stay faithful, but He doesn't seem to be using all that I believe I'm capable of. And He isn't explaining why. He has been quiet in the past, but the silence in this circle seems to be much longer than the previous ones. Sometimes it feels like I'm blindly wandering through the dark, trying to find my way as best as I can with little to no guidance from Him.

Sometimes I've even wished I could just walk away from my belief in God. But the truth is, I'm in too deep. I've seen too much. I've seen God work in my life far too much to just walk away. I think lots of us can relate to Peter's response when people were starting to walk away from Jesus after He said some really confusing things. Jesus turns and asks Peter, "Are you leaving, too?"

Peter essentially says, I've got nowhere better to go—I'm into this thing too deep. I know you have the words of life.[1] I can relate. As much as God confounds, confuses, and seemingly gives me the silent treatment, deep inside I know He is working—somehow, someway. To walk away would just be foolish.

The more people I talk to, the more I've found I'm not alone in this feeling. In fact, the longer we walk with God, the more silent He seems to become. We used to feel connected to God and really felt a sense that He was with us, but now we feel alone and maybe even abandoned. We wish we could get back to that place where we felt totally connected to Him. Those exciting first days of faith where He seemed to be always talking to us. The place where He gave us the best parking spot at the store right when we prayed for it. Or when He seemed to be swinging open endless doors of opportunity. But now…crickets.

Oftentimes, people are afraid to talk about this feeling because they've been told that God's perceived silence is their fault. Well-meaning people say things like: "If you'd just pray and read your Bible more, you wouldn't feel so disconnected." Or "Is there hidden sin in your life?" So we don't talk about the struggle and just get discouraged and hopeless or maybe even resentful.

Nothing can lead to despair and hopelessness quicker than feeling abandoned and forgotten by God. Dealing with sickness, hardship, and struggle is one thing. But feeling like God has forgotten you in the middle of the struggle can be unbearable.

Saint John of the Cross, a Spanish monk, described this experience we all face as "the Dark Night of the Soul." At some point, we all face our own dark night. It can go by all sorts of names: a desert experience, spiritual loneliness, a dry season, feeling abandoned by God. No matter what you call it, it's a horrible feeling. It's a time when God feels distant, maybe even cold. It brings some intense emotions to the surface as we wrestle with our beliefs and faith.

There's a story about Teresa of Avila complaining to God about her trials and His seeming absence. In response to her complaints, God replied, "Do not complain, daughter, for it is ever thus that I treat My friends."

Teresa replied: "Ah, Lord, it is also on that account that Thou hast so few!"[2] She basically says, "If this is how you treat Your friends, no wonder You have so few of them!"

It may feel a little irreverent to say it, but if you've followed Christ for a while, you've probably been disappointed and disillusioned with Him. You may even have thought He wasn't very godly at times—leaving you feeling abandoned and betrayed. We call out to Him, but He doesn't answer—at least not in the way we hoped He would. Doubts start to creep in. You start to wonder if this walk of faith is even worth it.

All this is normal. It's part of the journey. If you haven't felt a dark night of separation or confusion with God, there's a good chance the God you've been following is a god you created in your image. Because the true God is full of mystery. The more we know Him, the more we realize just how little we know or understand His ways. Dark Nights of the Soul aren't punishment. They're part of the process. When we understand the importance of the Dark Night of the Soul in the circular process of God's work, it can help us get the most from the season.

The dark night, the dark cave, is part of the process He uses to make us stronger. The cave is the opportunity to test our mettle and strength. One of my favorite Proverbs of Solomon is, "If you faint in the day of adversity, your strength is small."[3] My wife thinks it's bizarre that I like such a negative-sounding verse. But I don't take it as negative, because I read the verse this way: if you face adversity and make it through (even if you're a bit beat up on the other side), you are way stronger than you think you are.

Hard times reveal strength. Anyone can survive easy times. Maturity and depth come from holding on in spiritually dark times. You don't get spiritually strong when there's sunshine and unicorns and angels bringing good tidings of great joy all around you. You get spiritually strong when you're faced with doubt and uncertainty and choose to hold onto truth that is deep inside of you. That's faith. Faith is holding on to truth even when it seems like the truth isn't true.

The dark cave is the final exam. It's the test before the next level. In the words of A. W. Tozer: "Are you willing to take the test? If you pass, you can expect to be elevated to a new level in the

Kingdom. For He brings us through these tests as preparation for greater use in the Kingdom. You must pass the test first."[4]

When we take a test in school, it has questions and problems that we have to prove we can work through using the truth we've internalized on the journey up to this point. Tests reveal whether you really know the material without the teacher feeding you the answers. During a test, the teacher sits in the corner quietly as you prove that you really know the material you've been learning. The teacher doesn't feed you answers. That defeats the purpose. I shared the old Zen proverb that when a student is ready, a teacher appears. But the whole proverb is: "When the student is ready, the teacher will appear. When the student is truly ready, the teacher will disappear."

What if God's silence in the dark cave moments of testing isn't punishment? What if it's a sign of His confidence? He believes you're prepared. If you start to see God's silence as His confidence that you're able to pass the test in front of you, it could lead to a whole new perspective in that dark cave. Like roots growing strong in the darkness of the soil, the dark cave of God's silence can be your greatest catalyst for growth.

Keep Your Eyes on the Gardener

For years, I tried growing basil. But I couldn't keep a plant alive for more than a few weeks. The plant would grow, I'd pick off a few leaves here and there, thinking that the less I took the stronger the plant would be, but then it would die. I started doing some research and found that if you want a massive harvest of basil, you have to constantly prune the tops of the stems as they grow. If you cut the tops to keep it from growing high, it will grow huge amounts of rich, thick leaves. It will also last a long, long time.

Growing strong and healthy plants requires constant pruning. Our spiritual growth is no different. Jesus compares the spiritual growth process to the physical growth process when He says, "Every branch in me that does not bear fruit he takes away, and every branch that does bear fruit he prunes, that it may bear more fruit."[5] Basically, you are getting pruned one way or another. If you aren't doing anything of value, you're getting pruned. If you're producing fruit, be prepared to get pruned so you can produce even more. Being a rich source of life requires pruning back anything that isn't supporting the fruit you're capable of producing.

The Dark Night of the Soul can feel like being pruned. The spiritual support systems you depended on—feeling God's presence, confidence, and certainty in what you believe—are all stripped away, and you enter the cave empty-handed and alone. It's a lonely and disorienting road.

When the pruning begins, it's easy to focus on what God is using to prune you—His silence, feeling abandoned and alone, the person who is making your life miserable, the rejection, the pain—but we have to keep our perspective lifted. Keep your eyes off the pruning shears and focus on the one doing the pruning. Trust that whatever He's cutting away in your life is something keeping you from being all you have the potential to be. If God cuts something or someone out of your life, you can be certain it was something that was holding you back.

God's pruning in the dark cave is a gift, even if it doesn't feel like it at the time.

His pruning can help us conquer our need for affirmation from others, our dependence on turn-by-turn instructions from on high, and getting our sense of worth from what we own, know, or do. The Master knows what will keep you from producing your greatest work. If you can keep your perspective on the big, circular picture, you can have faith that whatever God is stripping away in the cave is a gift to help you let go of anything that is limiting you from becoming all He knows you can be.

And the truth is, more often than not, what is limiting us is nothing outside of us. What's limiting us are the mindsets, attitudes, fears, and hurts inside us. This is where the journey goes internal. What's outside of you becomes less important than what's happening inside of you. In the words of Michael Meade, "In hard times, inner changes must precede changes to outer circumstances."[6] In the dark cave, we tend to realize that the true struggle is within us.

The Victory of Surrender

The book of Job is most likely one of the oldest books of the Bible. Which I think is quite telling, because Job is the story of man's relationship to God's mysterious and sometimes painful ways. Humans have been confounded by God's ways since the beginning of time. Job goes through a truly dark cave where he loses pretty much everything he has worked for up to that point. His family. His wealth. His health.

His friends come to console him. They offer all sorts of explanations for his dark night. Some say it's hidden sin. Others say it's fate. Some say it's random. Job is bewildered. He was serving God to the best of his ability and then all these horrible things happened to him. His faith seems to be shaken. He starts asking what he did wrong.

Near the end of the book, God shows up and starts talking. But in chapter after chapter of God's response, He doesn't offer any real answers to Job's questions. He just starts firing off questions—like a teacher does with a test. It's all one-sided. God doesn't seem bothered by Job's questions, but He does rebuke Job's friends for their simplistic answers to the situation. In the end, Job humbly acknowledges, "I have uttered what I did not understand, things too wonderful for me, which I did not know. Hear, and I will speak; I will question you, and you make it known to me. I had heard of you by the hearing of the ear, but now my eye sees you."[7]

Job's moment of clarity and comfort comes when he acknowledges his limited understanding of the bigger picture. In the words of G. K. Chesterton, "Indeed the book of Job avowedly only answers mystery with mystery. Job is comforted with riddles; but he is comforted."[8] Oftentimes, peace comes not with clarity but with embracing mystery.

This seems to be the pattern of most enlightenment. It comes when we feel least certain. Enlightenment comes when we find contentment with mystery. And that's the victory in the cave. Emerging victorious from your decisive battle in the cave will often feel more like an act of surrender than of victory. That's the strange paradox of the dark cave. Winning victory over the enemy in the cave rarely looks like we thought it should. In fact, more often than not, it feels like a loss. Loss of capacity. Loss of autonomy. Loss of freedom. Loss of security. Even loss of life. That's the paradox.

Ultimate victory in the walk of faith looks a lot like surrender.

Every time we surrender more of our life to God's plan and purpose, we win greater victory. Jesus surrendered to His Father's will and won the victory. The same is true for us. Our surrender to His plan is where we find meaning and purpose. "Thanks be to God, who always leads us as captives in Christ's triumphal procession and uses us to spread the aroma of the knowledge of him everywhere."[9] When we feel defeated by the mystery of God and surrender to that mystery, letting Him lead us wherever He sees fit, there's peace. This is also when we actually start to have something to offer the world.

The Beatitudes indicate that blessing is reserved for those who are in a position of loss and surrender. Blessed are the poor in spirit, those who mourn, the meek, those who are hungry and thirsty. Surrendering to God's will and ways is the ultimate victory.

You aren't surrendering your personality or who you are at your core. Remember, God made you exactly who you are for His purposes. He likes how He made you. He just wants you to become all He made you to be. The goal of surrender is transformation into His glorious image.[10] Surrender is allowing *Him* to use all of you—your personality, your talents, and even your pain—for His purposes.

I tend to believe it's not even a matter of giving up your will, as much as it is submitting your will to God's will. (Completely letting go of your own will would make you no longer human—you'd be a mind-numb robot.) We don't give up our will. We willingly surrender it to God's will. Like Jesus, we say, "Not my will, but Your will be done." In that act of submission, we find the victory.

The victory in the dark cave may feel like death of part of who we are. But in that death, we actually find total freedom and victory. Death, then resurrection. That's the pattern. Before we can be resurrected to something new and glorious, first we must die.

Often, victory feels like going backwards. We feel like half the person we used to be. During a dark cave in my life a few years ago, I wrote this little poem to describe the feeling:

In my youth I was confident;
Now I'm not so sure.
In my youth I had so much to offer;
Now, well…I wonder.
In my youth I was bold;
Now I look before I leap.
In my youth I felt complete;
Now, half the man I used to be.
In my youth He began a process;
A thorough work for sure.
He broke the confident man I was;
Down to this weak thing on the floor.
Couldn't he have used me when I had so much to give?
Back before He ruined me
And strained me through His sieve.
My confidence is returning,
But its foundation is the Truth;
That the process that He started, He will follow through.
Relentless, He will make us into who we need to be,
Though painful, hard, and humbling;
Pure Gold He wants to see.

Pure gold only emerges from intense heat and straining. It's a deep work of foundational transformation. If we'll embrace this purifying part of the journey, we'll emerge from the cave stronger and wiser because we've realized the decisive battle is fought inside us—not outside us. We'll surrender more to His will. And that will be victory. Meister Eckhart was known to have said it this way: "The outward work will never be puny if the inward work is great."

Jesus lived that pattern of surrender and death and got the victory of glory. When we live the same pattern, He passes some of that glory on to us.

The Victory in the Cave

When we left Mexico, I felt defeated. But the more time passes, the more I see just how important all the lessons I learned there were. I wish I would have handled all the stress and conflict better. But I learned so much about who I am, and am not, during that time. I learned that I needed to deal with some deep anxiety and anger inside of me that had come to the surface. I learned the importance of relationships and communication with difficult people. I learned that God is always leading, even when He seems silent. The list of things I learned continues to grow as God's plan for my future unfolds.

I believe the same is true for your story.

The message God is preparing you to share requires depth and strength. You can't lead people somewhere you haven't been. As Henri Nouwen put it, "The great illusion of leadership is to think that man can be led out of the desert by someone who has never been there."[11] In our desert season, our dark cave, we face off with what we'd rather avoid. There will be something we're required to surrender in the dark cave. When we surrender, we win the battle. We deepen our message.

You'll probably feel like half the person you used to be. You may feel like you know less than you knew before the struggle. You won't feel quite as certain about some things anymore. But that's okay. You'll be more comfortable with not knowing, and you'll also become free from illusions and fear and your determination that things need to be a certain way. When you say, like Jesus, "Not my will, but Your will be done," you will find freedom and ultimately a new perspective. It may even feel like a rebirth. A new you.

The dark night of the soul comes just before revelation.
When everything is lost, and all seems darkness,
then comes the new life and all that is needed.

—*Joseph Campbell*

The Resolution

*If you are wise, you will not look upon the long period
of time thus occupied in actual movement as the mere
gulf dividing you from the end of your journey, but
rather as one of those rare and plastic seasons of your
life, from which, perhaps, you may love to date the
moulding of your character—that is, your very identity.*

—*Alexander William Kinglake*

After we closed the ministry, gave everything away, packed up
our stuff, and moved out, I was left wondering what to do. It
all happened so fast that I was scrambling to figure out whether we
should just move back home or try something new. We were fully
funded missionaries who were now without a mission.

I called my dad, who happens to run a missions agency that
oversees hundreds of different ministries around the world. He said,
"Well, where do you want to go?"

I found that question odd. I hadn't wanted to go to Mexico, but
God made it clear that was where I needed to be. "Does it really
matter where I want to go? God's supposed to tell me, right?"

He laughed. "Well, sometimes God gives a specific call. But oftentimes I believe His will is *whatever*. Delight yourself in the Lord and he will give you the desires of your heart."

"Whatever? But shouldn't I feel called there?"

"Maybe. Or maybe the desire to go there is the call. Where would you want to go?"

I had always wanted to visit South America. Dad fired off a few opportunities he knew of. One in particular—starting a cafe and church in Peru—really caught my attention.

Long story short, after a few calls, we decided to move to Cuzco, Peru, high in the Andes Mountains—sight unseen—to help start an English-language church and cafe.

When we got to Peru, I literally could not believe how wonderful it was. The weather was dry and cool. The people were kind and welcoming. No one was threatening my life. Cops weren't chasing me. I didn't have to constantly repair broken things. For the first few weeks, it all felt a bit too easy. Sure, it had some challenges, but it was nothing compared to what we had just experienced in Mexico. At times I felt guilty. *Shouldn't life be harder than this?*

I look back now and wish I would have enjoyed that season of calm a little more. I felt like I had just wasted a year of my life in Mexico, so I was in a rush to get moving on our next project — starting the church and cafe. I never really took time to reflect and process what we had just experienced in Mexico. (I'm finally doing it now, writing this book!)

In every season, after facing a series of challenges, going through the dark cave and surrendering to the new way of seeing the world, there comes a moment of resolution. Frodo returns to the Shire.

Dorothy goes back to Kansas. The hero starts a journey back home. In story writing it's called the dénouement: the events following the climax of a drama or novel in which a resolution or clarification takes place.[1] You've faced the dark cave and emerged transformed. Circumstances around you may or may not have changed, but the most important thing is: you've changed. The way you see the struggle has changed. The way you see the world has changed. You are a different person than you were when you started the journey.

The dénouement, or resolution, is a part of the circle that holds a lot of grace and revelation—if we'll slow down and embrace it. Too often, we're so anxious to get back to "normal" or make up for lost time that we never slow down to really evaluate what we've experienced. Who wants to revisit or think about all the struggles we just went through? Shouldn't we put the past behind us and just move on?

Again, the answer is yes...and no. We should move forward. The danger is, if we never slow down to evaluate the journey to this point, we're very prone to miss out on the lessons we need to learn. It's possible to walk into a new season and miss what we needed to learn in the previous circle. If we don't properly process the experience, we can emerge from it a little more bitter, paranoid, and tainted about life. If we take the time to process and heal, we'll gain more wisdom and expand our capacity to love God and others.

Experience isn't the best teacher. Evaluated experience is the best teacher. If you really want the full benefits of the preparation in each season, you must take time to evaluate the season—what went right, what you could have done better. Typically, this means acknowledging that the season has changed you. You are a different person. If you can be grateful for the change and keep

yourself from becoming numb or resenting what you just experienced, you'll begin to see the world in a new light. You'll gain the
new perspective you need from the circle. Most importantly, you'll
grow a little wiser. So let's talk about how to make the most of a
time of resolution.

Give It Time to Heal

A friend of mine lost his wife to an extremely rare medical
condition that put her in the hospital for months before she eventually passed away. It was a very dark cave for him. The loss was
tragic. What made it worse was that he had been certain God was
going to heal her. People from all over the world had "prophesied"
that God would heal her in a miraculous way. He was holding on
to that hope. But she died after a long struggle.

I watched my friend go into hyperdrive the moment he buried
his wife. He sold the house, gave away all her things, moved his
family, and within just a few short months was remarried to a
woman who was also grieving the loss of a spouse. Eventually, they
got divorced.

My friend never took time to slow down, create some space to
grieve, and just sit in the reality of his new world. And I understand
why. Who wants to sit in the pain of losing the love of your life? I
can't even imagine what that would feel like. He wanted things to
go back to something resembling normal. Problem was, life had
completely changed. And so had he. The frantic desire to get things
back to "normal" created chaos and fear in his kids and even more
stress in the end.

My friend's response was similar to what a lot of us do after we've emerged from challenges and the dark cave. It's natural to want to just pick yourself up, dust yourself off, and act like nothing ever happened. Like a kid playing, we may have some scraped knees and bruises, but there's no time to slow down and evaluate. Throw some dirt on it, and let's get back to doing something! Let's move along.

There is value in moving forward in spite of being hurt. In fact, oftentimes, that's our only option. However, it's also important that we give wounds a fighting chance to heal by alleviating some stress on them. A broken bone will never heal correctly if it constantly has pressure on it. But if it has time to rest with minimal pressure on it, it can (and usually will) heal back stronger. If it doesn't get a rest, it won't heal correctly. Just like our physical bodies, our soul (mind and emotions) needs some time to heal.

We talked about antifragile systems that actually gain from disorder and stress a few chapters ago. But antifragile systems only get stronger when they're given time to recover. The battles you've faced left a mark—they probably even wounded you. To gain the full benefit of those wounds, you'll need to slow down and give yourself some space to recover and find some resolution. You probably won't be able to just shut down your life and spend time sitting in your room to process a difficult season. But you can do things to take some pressure off specific areas of your life.

I see lots of people jump into a new relationship after messy divorces. They'll say things like, "The marriage has been over for a long time. It's just a matter of paperwork now." They feel like they've wasted some good years of their life in a bad marriage and now they want to dive back in, full force, and find their soulmate.

Problem is, even a "clean" divorce takes a heavy emotional toll. There are lots of complicated and painful variables that lead to divorce. It takes time to evaluate and process those variables.

If you really want resolution after heartbreak, you'll need to give your heart some time to heal. You'll have to leave emotional space and just spend some time being single. Otherwise, you're prone to carry those unhealed wounds into another relationship, which could potentially sabotage your success in the future. I love a line I've heard Richard Rohr use on many occasions: "If we do not transform our pain, we will most assuredly transmit it." We have to take the time to let our pain be processed and transformed.

The resolution comes right after the dark cave. It's a moment of grace and peace. Don't rush back into the fray. A new season is coming. But for now, lean into the grace God has given you right now. Look deep inside. Process as much as you can. Sit in the discomfort (or the calm). Your success in the next season will be greatly dependent on correctly processing in this season. The journey to this point made an impact. Recognize that impact. But through processing the pain, we're able to transform it. When we transform the pain, it becomes part of the message we have to share with the world. God will actually use your wounds to give you your next mission. In the words of A. W. Tozer, "It is doubtful whether God can bless a man greatly until he has hurt him deeply."[2]

Getting Over It

A few years ago, my wife and I went through a really challenging time. In a very short period, I got hurt by a pastor, ended up having to leave my job at a church, had to move out of my dream home, and found myself in a very dark cave. My whole life got turned upside down. I was mad at the church and pastors and God. I got some counseling and walked through the process of forgiving the guy who hurt me, but I still couldn't shake this depressed feeling I had about the whole thing.

Through a series of random events, I found myself in Venezuela helping a guy purchase a sailboat. While I was there, I realized this was my chance to check something off my bucket list. I went to visit Angel Falls, the highest waterfall in the world. It cascades off one of the giant *tepuis*—flat-topped mountains unique to the Gran Sabana region of South America. After saying goodbye to my buddy at the airport, I hired the pilot of a single-engine Cessna to take me deep into the jungle. We bounced down on a small landing strip in a clearing in the jungle. From there we took a dugout wooden canoe on a long journey up the Churun River. At times, we had to carry the boat around dangerous sections of rapids. Eventually we arrived at a small, stony beach. We tied our canoes up on the riverbank, hiked through dense jungle, and made our way to the base of the falls. The closer we got, the denser the spray from the nearly kilometer-high waterfall became. That night we slept in hammocks near the falls and roasted a pig on a handmade spit. It was pretty much my idea of the perfect trip.

Somewhere in the middle of that amazing experience I had an *aha!* moment. I heard something inside me say, *Are you ready to get over your mental fog now and move ahead?* Something clicked in my mind in that moment. I remember looking around at where I was and realizing that I never would've been able to take a trip like that if I was still at that job. That pastor hated it when I took vacation for more than just a few days. (In fact, he had offered my job

to someone else while I was on vacation!) If I was honest, I had been
dying inside a little bit each week while sitting in boring staff meet-
ings. The way it all ended was horrible and painful, but I never
would have been able to take that trip or walk through lots of other
doors that were opening had that not happened. I realized it was
time to pick myself up and move on. So, I did. Right there in
Venezuela. There wasn't a bunch of crying or emotion (that had all
come before in counseling), it was just a moment when I knew I
needed to get over it. I wasn't going to let what happened define me
anymore.

In every circle and season, you'll have to do some processing
after the struggle. As you process, a moment will arise when you'll
have the opportunity to hold onto the past and the injustice of it
all, or let go of it, seize the grace to overcome the past, and move
into the next phase.

May I suggest you seize the grace and move forward.

Let go of the hurt and pain. Refuse to be defined by what happened. Yes, it had an impact. Yes, you may have many justifiable
reasons to be angry and disappointed with people and God for the
challenges and struggles you had to face. But if you stay in that
place, you'll never gain the benefits of what those struggles have
built into you. You might even miss out on some amazing opportunities that are opening around you. Get your heart clear of the
hurt about what happened to you, and move on. Let it go.

Letting It Go

Every circle comes with wounds we sustained on the
journey—betrayal, father or mother wounds, rejection, physical

limitations. We've all been hurt. People have hurt us. Organizations and the church have hurt us. We've hurt ourselves. You might even feel like God hurt you. If you don't acknowledge that you need some healing, you'll constantly be bumping up against the same struggles in your life. And you'll probably respond to them the same way you did in the past—which will lead to more wounds.

God's answer to the hurt of the world was Himself. He gave His Son—God in the flesh—to offer forgiveness and reconciliation. I believe forgiveness is the way we break free from the hurt of the past, present, and future.

I talk a lot about the process of forgiveness in my book *Love Slows Down*, so I won't go in depth here. But for now, here are two really important things I've learned about forgiveness:

1. Forgiveness is a decision. It doesn't depend on some feeling or a confession from those who hurt you. It's your decision to release them from the hurt they caused you. You can forgive right now, even if they never admit their guilt. Forgiveness is a decision to set yourself free.

2. Forgiveness is a one-time decision, but you have to remind yourself of your decision over and over. Whenever we've been hurt, we have to grieve what was taken from us—our innocence, our hopes and dreams. Grief is more like a spiral than a straight line. (There's that circular pattern of life again!) The feelings associated with the hurt will return, even after you've decided to forgive, but you remind yourself of your decision. Eventually, the space between the feelings of pain will get further and further apart. You'll just remember the event with a sense of peace.

Forgiveness is the first step toward letting go of the negative feelings we have about any season. I'm convinced that it's not until we forgive and let go of the hurt that we begin to get perspective on any given season and the good God can bring from it.

Forgiveness is a lifelong skill we must develop, because as the circles repeat in our lives, growing us into who we need to become, we will experience more hurt. But, like we talked about in the first chapter, that pain can point to despair, or it can point to your destiny. You have to decide what to do with the pain. Pain points us toward our destiny when we choose to let go of the hurt and move forward in forgiveness.

Even after you heal, you'll probably walk with a limp. My friend who lost his wife will never get her back—that's his limp. He'll always have a wound related to that loss. Divorce is a wound that won't go away. Dealing with a life-altering illness may be the limitation you walk around with for the rest of your life. Beating an addiction but always having the temptation may be your limp. A major failure or financial setback may be your limp. We all walk with a limp that we carry with us in some area. But that's okay. Your limp—your wound—is the very thing God will often use to help you find the deep meaning and purpose in your life.

Walking with a Limp

My grandfather grew up in poverty in the bayous of southern Louisiana. When he was a young child, he contracted polio and lost his ability to walk. The Shriners Hospital paid for a surgery that fused his knee and gave him some mobility, but for his entire life, he had to use a cane. Eventually, he had to use a wheelchair. He became very successful in business but was always so concerned about his safety and ability to be mobile that he hardly ever stopped moving. Always buying or selling land. Always trying to keep a safety net around him to compensate for his limp. He regularly had two or three backup mobility devices in his garage, just in case.

The last months of his life, he was bedridden. It was a dark cave for him. During his final weeks, I watched him surrender to where he was. I'll never forget sitting next to him in his bed, just a few days before his death, when he said, "Joël, God has taught me more about who He is while I was laying in this bed for the last few months than I think I've learned in my entire life." My grandpa was constantly running, trying to prove he wasn't limited. He was always trying to provide and make sure he would be safe. He didn't want to show any weakness. But the last few months of his life forced him to slow down. God was working—right until the end—helping my grandfather process a lifetime of seasons. God will accomplish his work, to the very end. But I'm convinced that we don't have to wait until the very end to make some sense of life.

If you want to find some meaning beyond just survival right now (which is exactly what I hope this book is helping you do), acknowledge your reality and lean into it. Don't despise the wounds and the limp you've gotten on the journey. Like my grandfather, we all tend to see our limp as the greatest threat to our security, connection, or control. It's a sensitive spot that leaves us vulnerable— something we need to compensate for. But it's our limp that God uses to give us a message for the world.

There's an odd story in Genesis where Jacob, the grandson of Abraham the patriarch, demands a blessing from an angel and ends up in a wrestling match with him for it. Jacob does get the blessing, but in the process, the angel permanently injures Jacob's hip. Then the angel (who, it turns out, is God Himself) changes Jacob's name to Israel, which means "wrestles with God." Jacob got his blessing in the very moment he got a wound he would carry for the rest of his life.

With that wound, he also got a new identity. He became Israel and stepped into fulfilling his role in the promise given to his ancestor Abraham of making a great nation. He was part of completing the work of his father, but first he had to enter the battle and emerge with a wound.

I think this story is a picture of what happens in our lives.

Every circle will come with wounds. Wounds people gave us. Wounds we gave ourselves. Others are wounds that God Himself allowed to be inflicted. But in the strange irony of God's redemption, those wounds are often what He uses to accomplish His purpose in your life. The blessing you want in your life will often come with a deep wound that causes you to limp. The wound you got in the dark cave may actually be precisely what God uses to give you a new perspective.

What if you saw your wounds as the grace of God? Yes, a limp feels limiting. Sometimes our wounds make us feel like half the person we used to be. But what if they're what God wants to use as the source of your strength, so you can truly say, "I am content with weaknesses, insults, hardships, persecutions, and calamities. For when I am weak, then I am strong."[3] Talk about a perspective shift!

In Thornton Wilder's short play, *The Angel that Troubled the Waters*, a man is sitting by a healing pool waiting for an angel to stir up the waters so he can jump in and be healed of a flaw he doesn't like about himself. The angel appears, stirs the water, but then refuses to let the man enter the pool for his healing. The man protests, begging the angel to let him in. But the angel says: "Without your wounds, where would your power be? It is your melancholy that makes your low voice tremble into the hearts of men and women. The very angels themselves cannot persuade the wretched and blundering children on earth as can one human being broken on the wheels of living. In Love's service, only wounded soldiers can serve."

Your wounds have the power to speak life to others. Your wounds give you a message to share with the world.

Is it possible that the thing you're most ashamed of—the thing you hate the most from your past—is what God wants to use as part of redeeming the world from darkness? In the words of Rumi, an ancient mystic, "The wound is the place where the Light enters you." What if the limp you try to hide—the wound—is the very thing that will open the door to make an impact in this world? As Robert Bly said it, "Where a man's wound is, there he finds his genius."[4]

What about the parts of your story—the circles—you still can't make sense of or bring any closure to? You've tried to find resolution, you even pulled back and spent some time pondering, but it's not bringing any peace. I've been there, and I like what Rainer Rilke has to say about those unresolved parts:

> Be patient toward all that is unsolved in your heart and try to love the questions themselves, like locked rooms and like books that are now written in a very foreign tongue. Do not now seek the answers, which cannot be given you because you would not be able to live them. And the point is, to live everything. Live the questions

now. Perhaps you will then gradually, without noticing it, live along some distant day into the answer.[5]

A New Perspective

Whenever I lead hiking teams around the world, I always leave time at the end of the trip for a debriefing. I know that as soon as the team gets home, life is going to hit them in the face and they're going to get really, really busy again. My friend Mark Batterson developed a formula I really love: Change of Pace + Change of Place = Change of Perspective. On our trips, people tend to get a new perspective, and I want them to really process it. But that won't happen unless they take some time to reflect. It's really easy to go through a potentially life-changing experience but miss some important lessons from it.

While I was growing up in Guatemala, our family brought teams from around the world to serve in some very poverty-stricken regions. The last night of the trip, we always had a debrief with team members about their experience. It wasn't uncommon for people to say things like, "It was so wonderful to see all those people living in their primitive environment without a care in the world." This was baffling to hear, because they had just seen people who were literally starving and living on dirt floors, being infected with all sorts of preventable diseases because of lack of sanitation. But the team members saw what they wanted to see. They saw it like Disney World, where characters come out dressed in native garb and put on a show for you then go back to their comfy homes. The team members didn't see the reality of it. Without some guidance and evaluating what they had seen correctly, people could see abject poverty and leave without a true understanding of what they had just experienced.

If you don't take the time to evaluate an experience, you can miss very important lessons and realities. Or worse yet, you can gain a completely flawed perspective on the experience because you don't have a full picture of what actually happened. This is why reflecting after some time has passed is so important in each circle or season of life. It's also why it's important to bring people in on the process—counselors, pastors, priests, and friends who can help bring an outside perspective. Without a proper interpretation of what happened, you won't gain the full benefit of the experience and training you received.

After the victory in the dark cave, you emerge with a story to tell. Now you start the journey home. Of course, home will be different. You'll be different. But you're returning with a message, a story to tell. But first, you must evaluate your experience. Leave yourself time to process and heal a bit. Don't just jump back into another battle. A new circle will begin soon enough.

For now, receive this window of grace to process what has happened. There will be other challenges ahead, but be intentional about slowing down to process the experience. Because the experience has changed you, you have a new perspective.

You've changed.

You've grown.

Armed with a new perspective, your greatest impact is still ahead.

When everything is a beginning, every end is bearable.

—*John Shea*

The New Perspective

And we all, with unveiled face, beholding the glory of the Lord, are being transformed into the same image from one degree of glory to another. For this comes from the Lord who is the Spirit.

—2 Corinthians 3:18

Transcend and include…this is the self-transcending drive…to go beyond what went before and yet include what went before…to open into the very heart of Spirit-in-action.

—Ken Wilber

Emily and I moved to the Andes Mountains. We started a church to reach spiritual seekers who came to Cuzco looking for enlightenment from shamans and indigenous spiritualists. To help with that mission, we started a cafe right on a central square in the art district called San Blas. All kinds of people from all over the world—from Ivy League professors to unkempt hippies in loose-fitting, white linen clothing—came through our doors. It was a completely different world from Mexico. I loved it!

And as far as I was concerned, I never wanted to revisit the Mexico experience. I still couldn't decide if the whole thing was one big failure—a negative mark on my permanent record—or just a huge waste of time. It was one big season where I was angry and afraid, and basically insane, for nearly a year. In contrast, this new adventure in Peru was a wonderful, successful experience. There were some challenges, but everything seemed to click. We had a constant flow of people from all over the world arriving to help. Our cafe was in a prime location, right in the middle of all the action of the ancient city. We had tangible evidence of success—a church, a cafe, some great friends that we made quickly. And none of them were threatening our lives! It was a new circle, but it was also a time of some resolution. If Mexico was a total failure, Peru felt like a total success.

But I can honestly say, looking back, that I grew way more in Mexico than I ever did in Peru. In the short-term, Peru felt like a win and Mexico felt like a total loss. But now, further down the road, I'm rethinking that perspective. I'm wondering if the real win happened in Mexico and the Peru experience was just a consolation prize God gave us in His grace. This is the nature of God's work. It's a slow work that reveals the plan over time. You just never know how good something might turn out to be when it's all said and done. The worst possible things can end up being the best possible things. In the words of King Solomon, "The end of a matter is better than its beginning, and patience is better than pride."[1]

Time tends to be the ultimate truth-teller. After time passes, we see much more clearly what is true and what is real.

A few years back, my dad had to confront someone in a meeting. Afterward I asked him, "How'd it go, Dad?"

He smiled. "We'll see. If things get better in the next few weeks, it went well. If not, it was a big waste of time."

We'll see. I'm convinced this is the best response to every season of life. What you've faced, or are facing right now, might feel like the worst thing that could ever happen to you.

But…we'll see.

The story isn't over yet. As G. K. Chesterton put it: "One of the most necessary and most neglected points about the story called history is the fact that the story is not finished."[2] As God slowly reveals His master plan, we'll see outcomes we never could have imagined. So for now, we have to withhold judgment on the exact nature of what we're dealing with. Full perspective will only come with time. Every circle of life finds meaning in the bigger picture, so to keep our life in proper perspective, we have to withhold judgment.

A Judgment Call

I'm a pretty black-and-white thinker by nature. So I used to laugh at spiritual hippie gurus in white linen clothes (lots of them came into our cafe in Peru) or inspirational self-help practitioners who would say, "Don't judge."

That's ridiculous! You have to judge some things. There are some things that are downright evil. Things like tyranny, abuse, and violence need to be judged as bad. Sitting around deciding to not judge those kinds of evils means you may actually become part of the problem.

But the Eastern mystics aren't the only ones who said not to judge. The Apostle Paul said something really uncomfortable and confusing that sounds pretty similar: "Therefore do not pronounce judgment before the time, before the Lord comes, who will bring to light the things now hidden in darkness and will disclose the purposes of the heart. Then each one will receive his commendation from God."[3]

Is Paul really telling us to not judge anything? Sort of. As with all complex things, the answer to judging what you see is nuanced. It's yes . . . and no. You should judge some things. But also, humility recognizes that our perspective is limited. We don't know the whole story. There's always more going on than what we see.

Many of the things we judge as definitively "bad" (and which may truly be bad at the time) might actually be something to which we should say, "We'll see." When you have an all-powerful God who can turn anything around for His purposes, it's quite possible that the worst possible thing right now could be something that becomes quite glorious. Joseph being sold into slavery was clearly bad, but it ended up saving his whole family. Jesus being unjustly murdered on a cross was horrible, but who would have known what was going to come from it—the salvation of the world.

The same is true for us.

How something turns out depends on lots of variables. And there is one variable that can overwhelm all others: divine intervention.

God makes bad things into good things all the time. Which to me, is the definition of real, ultimate power. If you can take bad things and make them good, take dead things and bring them to life, then you truly have ultimate, final power. When you have total control over how the story ends, you have true omnipotence. All bets are off when you're dealing with that kind of power. Nothing is impossible with that kind of power.

When that kind of power gets involved, "we'll see." It ain't over 'til it's over.

Now, I can already hear you saying, "That's great Joël, but I've got real problems, *right now*. I don't have time to just float through this without judging." I hear you. When life gets crazy, it's hard to sit back and go with the flow, waiting for time to work things out. You don't want to be naïve or fake it until you make it. You need something solid to hold onto. Which is what I hope this book is offering you. I want to help you keep your perspective lifted and recognize where you are in the pattern of God's work. That's how you can hold onto hope right now. Keep things in perspective as best as you can.

Know this: God did not bring you this far to ditch you. He has turned bad to good up to this point in your life and He will continue that redemptive work right now. Part of faith is learning to trust the process and pattern we've talked about in this book. God works in circles that prepare us for future glory. If it's not glorious, it's not the end.

What if what is definitively bad right now in your life is actually going to be good in the final analysis?

I know, I know. That kind of thinking can be a very slippery slope. It makes my black-and-white, wrong-and-right brain very uncomfortable. I'm not trying to mess with you or deconstruct your morality. I'm not trying to get you to be flippant about pain or suffering. But I do think it's important to shift your perspective. It goes back to what Paul said: "We look not to the things that are seen but to the things that are unseen. For the things that are seen are transient, but the things that are unseen are eternal."[4] There's always more going on than what we see. There's a higher reality—an eternal reality—in which God is orchestrating all things for His purposes, which work out to our benefit. God is determined to turn all things for His ultimate glory. We have to be patient and watch His pattern—His plan—unfold. Knowing God's ultimate power, we can repeat with confidence the words of Julian of Norwich, "All shall be well, and all shall be well, and all manner of thing shall be well."

So here's a question: If you really believed that God was turning all things into something that brings Him glory and brings meaning and purpose to your life, what would that do to your perspective right now?

All things: the health issue, the marriage problems, the financial struggle, the injustice, the betrayal, the political situation. What if you really believed that "by him all things were created, in heaven and on earth, visible and invisible, whether thrones or dominions or rulers or authorities—all things were created through him and for him. And he is before all things, and in him all things hold together"?[5] How would you begin to see your life and the world around you?

As you evaluate a season of life over time, like layers of an onion, the deeper realities and truths begin to reveal themselves. Oftentimes, the very thing that seemed like the worst possible fate becomes a destiny-changing circumstance that vastly improves your life—after time passes. What if you're in the middle of one of those moments right now?

If my time in Mexico was a test, I made a D (if that!). And I had a bad attitude on top of it all. I wish I had handled it better, but it revealed areas of my life where I needed to grow and mature. God, by His grace, worked some things out of me and into me that I needed to learn. I eventually ended up writing a book about how to deal with anger and anxiety—things I learned in the bootcamp of Mexico. All the building and repair skills I learned by fixing things prepared me for the retreat center and cabins I'm currently building in the hills of Texas. The really wild thing is, while in Mexico, I started writing a book about perspective—right in the middle of not having any perspective on what was really happening. But the circle came back around, and I'm writing about it now, with the benefit of seeing in hindsight what God was working in me.

You will find the same to be true in your story as you look back. God was preparing you for your greatest work. Every circle is a journey "to grow up in every way into him who is the head, into Christ, from whom the whole body, joined and held together by every joint with which it is equipped, when each part is working properly, makes the body grow so that it builds itself up in love."[6] There's a unifying purpose in all God's work in our lives: growing into love is the goal.

Healthy Things Grow

My five-year-old daughter is obsessed with how big and how old she is. She always wants us to measure her by standing her next to a poster we have on her door. She talks about what she'll do when she's older. She gets into discussions with other kids about who is bigger and smarter and faster. There's something deep within us that drives us to grow and be bigger, better, and faster. In fact, when kids are born, doctors regularly measure those children to make sure they're keeping the proper pace. If a child isn't growing physically, it's usually the first sign they aren't healthy in some way.

We're all on our own journey in life, moving at our own pace. However, there are some growth markers that, if they aren't being met, should give us reason for concern. For followers of Christ, the measuring stick of growth is becoming more like Him. Christ was the embodiment of love. When it comes to spiritual growth, age and experience don't necessarily equal maturity. Love is the primary measuring stick for spiritual maturity. So I tend to believe that evaluating whether a season was a success or failure can come down to one question: Did we become more loving?

Defining what is truly love can be tricky. Sometimes love looks like going along with someone and picking them up time after time. Other times, the most loving thing is to allow someone to reap the harvest of their decisions, then be there to walk with them through rebuilding. Love can look like strict boundaries sometimes and it can look like no boundaries at other times—which is why we have to depend on our Guide to show us what love looks like in each season. I like M. Scott Peck's articulate definition of love: "Love is the will to extend one's self for the purpose of nurturing one's own or another's spiritual growth."[7] Navigating the loving path takes humility, courage, and constant vigilance. Love has lots of faces. "Love is patient and kind; love does not envy or boast; it is not arrogant or rude. It does not insist on its own way; it is not irritable or resentful; it does not rejoice at wrongdoing, but rejoices with the truth. Love bears all things, believes all things, hopes all things, endures all things."[8]

If living out that kind of love seems like an impossible task, then you probably have a correct understanding of what love really means. It's not easy. It's hard. It's impossible apart from being led by your Guide into an increasing awareness of who you are and who God is. The more you come to understand God and yourself, the more you realize how little you actually know and how much more room there is to grow.

If you ever hear someone talking about how loving they are, run! I've seen that those who are most immature love to talk about how mature, loving, and enlightened they are. But true maturity—walking in real love—actually creates the opposite results. Increasing awareness of truth should lead us to realize just how little we actually know. That kind of self-awareness leads to humility and meekness.

What Real Maturity Looks Like

One of the most profound explanations about what real maturity looks like tends to get lost in the confusing context of something Paul said: "Now about food sacrificed to idols: We know that 'We all possess knowledge.' But knowledge puffs up while love builds up. Those who think they know something do not yet know as they ought to know. But whoever loves God is known by God."[9]

Food sacrificed to idols? Umm, what does that have to do with knowledge and maturity?

It's easy to get lost in the weeds as Paul talks about people who are afraid to eat meat that was sacrificed to an idol. In his day, people would sacrifice an animal to a pagan idol, hoping to gain favor. Then the meat from that sacrificed animal would be sold for food. Lots of Christians refused to eat the meat because of what it had been used for. They felt it would taint them. Sounds like a bizarre situation to address, right? The best modern equivalent I can think of is this: Would you eat a pizza that a Satanist dedicated to the devil while making it? I would (it is pizza after all!), but some wouldn't. And I get why. Paul says that as mature Christians, we have freedom to eat that meat (or pizza), since we know that an idol isn't really a god.

So what does all this have to do with maturity?

Paul goes on to say that if someone we know is uncomfortable eating meat sacrificed to idols, then we should embrace them where they are and not eat that meat in their presence. He's saying we need to be patient with people at their current level of understanding. True maturity embraces people where they are and respects the circle of the journey they're currently walking. We humbly recognize that we're all on a journey of growth. This may mean sacrificing some of our freedom in Christ for those we love who haven't quite come to an understanding of that freedom.

He goes on to say that knowledge "puffs up." Knowledge can easily make us feel superior to those who don't know what we know. Once you know something, it's hard to remember what it was like not knowing it—that's the curse of knowledge. It's easy to feel more enlightened than those "small-minded people" and start to belittle and demean those who are on a different stage of the journey. But that's pride. The fact is, if you think that way about others, you really aren't mature at all. If you sit around thinking about how mature you are, you probably aren't. Real maturity is measured by your love and humility.

Jesus demonstrated this kind of enlightened maturity: "Who, being in very nature God, did not consider equality with God something to be used to his own advantage, rather, he made himself nothing by taking the very nature of a servant."[10] God in the flesh used His knowledge and power to serve, not to rule or belittle or condemn those who weren't enlightened to the fullness of truth. He came to our level and walked with us.

That is the definition of meekness. Meekness isn't weakness. Meekness is strength used for the benefit of another. It's love. Extending yourself for others. Jesus said, "The meek will inherit the earth."[11] We've all had that one teacher who took the extra time to truly teach us, rather than just saying, "Just read the book." They used their understanding of the material to guide us into understanding. We never forget that teacher. That teacher's investment lives on in us. That's the inheritance meekness brings. We use our strength to strengthen others, and that strength lives on in them.

When you walk in humility and meekness, you probably won't even realize you're doing it—but that's when you'll truly be mature. That's the nature of maturity: You arrive at maturity, but when you get there, it doesn't really matter to you anymore because you realize it was about the journey, not the destination. And then you arrive at a new level—a new perspective.

The Journey of Faith

I mentioned that when I was in Mexico, I started writing a book about perspective. I poured heart and soul into that book, hours and hours of my life. I was sure it was my *magnum opus*—my greatest work. When I was done with the book, I paid a writing coach to read the manuscript. The response she gave me was devastating. "This is a great start to your writing career. You got it all out on paper. Now you can go write your book."

What?! Now, I can go write my book? I could not conceive of writing another book. This had just taken every drop of knowledge and energy I had. I vowed to never be that discouraging to a new writer. But now that I've written a few books, I see just how right that coach was. That first book was a building block for me. Honestly, the book was horrible. It was preachy and self-righteous. It's embarrassing to even look at it now. I almost deleted it a while back, but I realized it was a great tool to keep me humble. There's nothing like looking back at where you came from to remind yourself that you haven't arrived yet.

After I "got it all out on paper," I realized I needed some coaching to get my writing on track. So I went to a writing conference. While I was there, a writing mentor of mine recommended a book that forever changed my view of the walk of faith. The book is called *The Critical Journey* by Janet Hagberg and Robert Guelich. In the book, they talk about the six stages in the life of faith.

Stage 1 is called the Recognition of God. "It's accepting the fact of the reality of God in our lives."[12] This is where our faith begins, with an understanding that we have a Creator who loves us and wants a relationship with us.

Stage 2 is the Life of Discipleship, where we begin to learn about God and gain a framework for how to live in harmony with His order and the world He created. We typically latch on to a handful of teachers and learn from them, seeing the truth they're teaching as the one-and-only way to see God and follow Him.

Stage 3, the Productive Life, is all about action and doing. We want to do something for God. We recognize talents and abilities God has placed in us and do our best to be good stewards of those by serving and action.

Stage 4 is the Journey Inward, where we begin to seek deeper answers about who we are and who God is. We've been following Jesus for a while but realize we still struggle with some things below the surface—fears, addictions, and hang-ups. We may not have seen the transformation we had hoped for by faithfully serving God. So we start to look a little deeper into ourselves.

The next stage is the Wall. This is the Dark Night of the Soul we talked about, the dark cave, where we face what Janet Hagberg calls "the mystery of our will meeting God's will face to face." The Wall looks different for each person and there is no simple path forward for folks in this stage. It's uncomfortable. We have to wrestle with God and give up our preconceived ideas about who He is and what He represents to us. We tend to want to run back to a previous stage—something familiar—a time when God and faith seemed simpler. This stage can be so uncomfortable and awkward that many feel they don't even have faith anymore. But if you can hang on and push through, you'll find it's all part of the process of growth.

Stages 5 and 6 involve total surrender to God and His will. In many ways, we begin to realize the journey has nothing to do with us—instead, "the only thing that counts is faith expressing itself through love."[13]

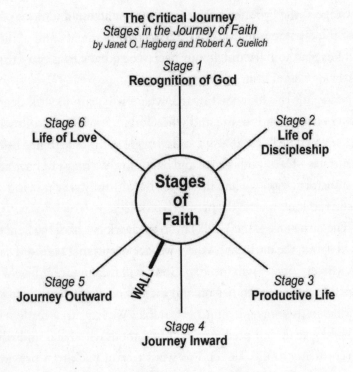

The Critical Journey
Stages in the Journey of Faith
by Janet O. Hagberg and Robert A. Guelich

It's really important to understand that this framework isn't some sort of checklist to accomplish and figure out how mature you are in your faith. Again, if you've concluded that you're mature, you probably aren't! In fact, I'm convinced we keep working our way around that circle over and over throughout the seasons of life—constantly growing and seemingly starting over. This framework is more of a tool for helping you gain perspective on the natural way that the journey of faith unfolds in our lives. (It's interesting that they also use a circle for their model.) It's a way to help you see that the challenges you're facing in that stage are part of the process. The stages are all necessary and build on each other, just like the stages in each circle and season.

We tend to have one home stage we go back to when life gets hard. But humility should always drive us to recognize there is more to know. We embrace each stage but never settle there. Many great spiritual teachers describe the process of growth as "transcend and include." Each stage has foundational value—we need each stage. As we grow in maturity, we transcend (go to another level) and include previous stages, recognizing their value in the journey. We need each stage and should never look down on what it took to get us where we are today. Never belittle where you came from; it was part of your journey. (In fact, if you believe you've transcended one stage but are constantly belittling where you came from or looking down on those in other stages as "unenlightened," I would question whether you have actually transcended it.)

(Side note: I think *The Critical Journey* also explains a lot of the conflict we have in the Body of Christ today. Some criticize churches who minister to those in the Recognition of God stage as being a "watered-down Gospel." Others criticize churches focused on the Journey Inward as being too morose or somber. Churches that focus on the Productive Life are criticized as being "uncontemplative" or "social justice warriors." But what if we need all those churches helping people in that specific phase of their journey? What if they aren't wrong but just a small part of the whole—each member doing its part in the Body of Christ? As we grow, we need different stages. Mature believers walk with and love people in every stage of the journey.)

Each circle increases our faith and, ideally, leads to a little more wonder and humility about how little we actually know. It's a journey of constant growth. Each transition to a new stage feels, well, new. Each phase leads us to a new perspective on God and His ways. And this process can be a bit disorienting.

Reorientation

Walter Brueggemann describes the sequence of growth and transition in the spiritual life as a pattern of: Orientation, Disorientation, and New Orientation. He was specifically writing about how each Psalm addresses one of these stages, but I think this is the process that every transition follows as well.

In seasons of Orientation, God and life just make sense. We feel totally connected with God and have a sense of clarity about His work in our lives. But when He calls you to another level of depth and maturity, the turning point shakes up your certainty and pushes you into the next stage.

Disorientation is the time of struggle that leads to the dark cave. It's the adventure (aka challenges) we talked about earlier in the book. It's the part of the circle where we're learning and being pushed beyond what we think we can handle. Oftentimes, the changes and new perspective can shake us so much that we want to get back to a "simpler" faith. We long for the certainty we used to have. We can actually start to worship foundational elements of the faith that were meant to be building blocks. We should respect and honor the building blocks that got us there, but if we stay camped out there, we'll never grow into the fullness of all God intends for us.

New Orientation is the resolution time when we begin to see God, the world, and ourselves from a new perspective. The more we grow in faith, the more we realize how little we know. But we learn to trust His divine hand leading us. We realize that the path we've walked was necessary to get us to this point. The adventure we got was the adventure we needed. We don't despise our story. We embrace it but always see it through the new perspective of God's redemption. He was leading us even when we didn't realize it. He is also leading those around us to growth. The truly meek and humble recognize this and use their strength and maturity to love others where they are on the journey. "Who is wise and understanding among you? Let him show by good conduct that his works are done in the meekness of wisdom."[14]

The new orientation (and a new perspective) always involves letting go but not despising what we have released. We go to another level but never forget where we came from. Our past was needed to get us to our present. But we don't stay in the past, we let it go and move ahead with the new perspective, always building on previous understanding. But remembering where we came from leads to humility and gives us patience for those who are on their own path of growth to understanding. We're all growing.

Humbly accepting ourselves and others right where we are is a hallmark of maturity. We accept where we are but move forward to all we could be. Even when we need to encourage others to step up to their potential, we stay humble, remembering that every stage of the journey was something we needed to get us to where we are today. We have not arrived. But we have a story to tell about the journey. We have a message to share and a problem that God has uniquely equipped us to address in this world.

And now, we get to the really good part.

God's love compels us outward to share the story of His work in our lives. Your message of God's work in your life is where you will find meaning and purpose in every circle of life you have lived. So let's look at how to nail down your message to share and problem to solve.

One cannot live the afternoon of life according to the program of life's morning; for what was great in the morning will be of little importance in the evening, and what in the morning was true will at evening become a lie.

—*Carl Jung*

The Message

He regards men not as they are merely, but as they shall be; not as they shall be merely, but as they are now growing, or capable of growing, toward that image after which He made them that they might grow to it. Therefore a thousand stages, each in itself all but valueless, are of inestimable worth as the necessary and connected gradations of an infinite progress.

—George MacDonald

Right after we moved back to the United States from our time in Mexico and Peru, I gave up on writing the book about perspective that I had been unable to write during our time south of the border. It just wasn't working. So I started writing another book about how to pursue impossible dreams, using a simple step-by-step process of starting small and charting out specific goals. That book, *Vision Map*, actually got published. It's the story of how God led me through a process of developing Summit Leaders, the outdoor leadership organization that started right about the time we moved to Mexico. The book has a happy ending where all my wildest dreams come true and I end up leading outdoor expeditions with prominent leaders around the world.

The thing is, there's a major part of that story I left out.

Between chapters sixteen and seventeen in that book, I experienced everything I wrote about in this book. I left that season out because it was too long of a story, and it felt completely irrelevant to that inspirational tale.

The season in Mexico didn't fit into the short-term perspective I had of my life at the time. But looking back, I see just how important that season was in the bigger picture. The part I left out of my story, in the long run, ended up becoming one of the most important experiences in my personal and spiritual development.

Not only was that season preparation, but it also perfectly positioned me where I needed to be to start the outdoor adventures. The first speaker who came with us just happened to want to do a hike on the Inca Trail to Machu Picchu, which starts right where I was launching our cafe and church in Cuzco. God positioned us right where we needed to be—but I didn't realize it until further down the road.

That season was also a building block for what would become the message I find myself sharing with people all the time. Through my struggle with fear and anger and trying to keep perspective, God had given me a unique experience that I want to make sure wasn't for nothing. As I've looked back over the last few circles of my life, I've seen a consistent message emerge, namely: stop unnecessary suffering (through wisdom) and find meaning in necessary suffering (through perspective). That's my message. Whenever I talk to people about how to conquer fear or deal with anger or keep their life in perspective, it all fits into that message.

You have a message, too.

It's more than likely that the part of your story that you'd rather leave out, skip over, or never revisit is where your greatest message and sense of meaning will be found—once you have the benefit of looking back with proper perspective. What happens in those seasons is not your identity. You are much more than what happened to you. But it was part of making you who you are today.

We limit ourselves when we can't separate who we are from what has happened to us. Richard Rohr talks about how important it is to turn your wounds into a message, rather than your identity: "It has been acceptable for some time in America to remain 'wound-identified' (that is, using one's victimhood as one's identity, one's ticket to sympathy, and one's excuse for not serving), instead of using the wound to 'redeem the world,' as we see in Jesus and many people who turn their wounds into sacred wounds that liberate both themselves and others."[1] You aren't your wounds, but your wounds carry a message.

What happens in the hard seasons has the potential to shape us in the greatest way—for better or worse. It's often the seasons when we felt weakest that God will use to make us strongest in the long run. If we can keep our perspective lifted and trust God is working all things together for good, it will keep us from turning bitter and paranoid and instead turn us into people who walk with wisdom, humility, and gratitude. Let your past be a reminder, not your identity. We have personal experience of God's work in our lives. A person with experience is never at the mercy of a person with a theory. Everything that has happened to you up to this point in your life has prepared you with a message. It has prepared you for your greatest work.

When I look back at my season in Mexico, I really wish I'd had a bigger perspective. I wish I would have looked for the bigger picture and stopped some of the unnecessary suffering of worry and anxiety and anger and trusted God more. I think it would have helped me chill out a bit instead of being constantly on edge. Because, truth is, there were some positive experiences in Mexico. I definitely should have handled it all better.

But even though I didn't respond in the best way, God has used it. God, in His goodness, takes even our failures and turns them into something that can help others, if we'll surrender our stories to Him.

So let me ask you a question: What part of your story would you rather leave out?

And here's an even bigger question: Is it possible that *that* specific season of your life holds the greatest power to impact the world with a story of God's redemption?

Maybe it's time to unpack your story—all of it—and connect the dots of God's work in everything that has happened to you. Maybe it's time to step into the power of meaning and purpose that God wants to give you.

Your personal story of God's work, even when you didn't realize He was working, has power. There is hope—you've seen it firsthand. There is salvation—you've experienced it. You aren't just talking theory or faking it until you make it—you have a direct revelation of God's work in your life. Let that light draw people to the goodness of God. "You are the light of the world. A city set on a hill cannot be hidden. Nor do people light a lamp and put it under a basket, but on a stand, and it gives light to all in the house. In the same way, let your light shine before others, so that they may see your good works and give glory to your Father who is in heaven."[2] There may be lots of shame you feel about your story, but there's also glory—God's glory—in your story. Let that glory overshadow any shame. Focus on telling people about the glorious work He has done in your life.

You have a unique message to share of God's faithfulness in your life. But that message isn't just for you. The world needs to hear it. You are called to use your message to love and serve others. Your message will help others find their calling and connect their own dots in the story God is writing with their lives. Your message will share His redemption. This is where we find a deep sense of meaning and purpose in our lives. When what we've experienced becomes a gift we can share with those who are struggling and hurting, our story takes on meaning.

From a Story to a Message

People regularly hand me books they've written about their life and ask me to give my opinion. I applaud them for writing out their stories. But often, these folks tell a long, intricate story of their personal life down to every detail. Sometimes they pay loads of money to have the book designed and printed.

I rarely get through those books.

I think there are two main reasons the books miss the mark and don't engage the reader. First, I think it's often because the author hasn't ever taken the time to really process what they learned from it. They haven't distilled down the essence of the story, which is why there are so many details. They still aren't quite sure what was most important. So they just put everything in the story. That's why I believe the framework in this book can be really helpful for you. It can help you connect the dots and bring clarity to the key elements of the story. You'll begin to see a consistent message God has been writing into your life.

Which brings me to the second reason I think many of the books I get handed aren't quite ready yet. Most only tell a story—they don't offer a message. There's no application or take-home for the reader. Maybe they'll offer some application at the very end. They assume you'll be fascinated and read through their long, complicated story. But unless they're an outstanding writer, that rarely happens. They've fallen into the trap of believing that their story alone is enough of an offering to people. But it's not. Your story holds most power when it offers a clear message of hope to others. There's a subtle difference between a story and a message, but it's super important.

Jesus saved the world through His death and resurrection. Then He sent His disciples on a mission: Go tell the world that God and humanity have been reconciled. Share the story everywhere and make disciples. Making disciples means showing people how to walk in the reality of what Christ did for us. Jesus sent them with that message. His life was a sacrifice that offered a message of hope to every person on Earth.

And that's the subtle difference.

If you want your story to become a message, you'll need a subtle shift in perspective. The power in your story comes when you surrender yourself and what has happened to you as a living sacrifice. That's when you stop focusing on your story being about you and let it be about the message of God's work in you. Your story is not for you—it's for others. Your life is a sacrifice. It's a way of showing them how Christ's work redeemed your story and how the same can be true for them. There's a passage in Revelation that talks about the saints being under attack from the enemy. It says, "They triumphed over him by the blood of the Lamb and by the word of their testimony."[3] God has done a work of redemption in your life. That testimony, telling the story of His work, has power to help others win their own battles. That's how your message helps solve a problem in the world.

If our personal stories aren't seen from the perspective of being an offering to the world, they can become a form of self-indulgence. They can become all about us, rather than about Christ's redemption. They'll get us stuck in a small circle of focusing on ourselves. The circles of our lives should push us outward, out of our self-focus and into the world at large. The more your story shifts toward doing whatever it takes to help others on their journey, the more it will come full circle and bring a sense of purpose. You shift from "Look at me, look at me!" to "Look at what God did in me and what He can do in *you* too!"

The Apostle Paul makes a strange statement to the Colossians when he says: "Now I rejoice in my sufferings for your sake, and in my flesh I am filling up what is lacking in Christ's afflictions for the sake of his body, that is, the church."[4] It sounds like Paul is saying that Christ didn't quite get the job done when He died. Like something was missing in what Jesus accomplished. Surely that can't be true. So what is Paul saying?

I think John Piper gives the best explanation I've heard of this when he writes:

> What's missing is the in-person presentation of Christ's sufferings to the people for whom he died. The afflictions are lacking in the sense that they are not seen and known among the nations. They must be carried by ministers of the gospel. And those ministers of the gospel fill up what

is lacking in the afflictions of Christ by extending them to others. Paul sees his own suffering as the visible reen-actment of the sufferings of Christ so that they will see Christ's love for them.[5]

What's true for Paul's story is true for yours.

When you shift your perspective and begin to see your suffering and trials as something God wants to use to tangibly express Christ's redemption to the world, it gives everything you've been through a whole new meaning. It wasn't for you. It was to show the world God's work in your life. That's how you can actually say you rejoice in your suffering. When you suffer well, understanding God will use all things for His glory, you actually get to be part of God telling the world His story of redemption through you. That's where meaning and purpose are found.

When you focus on using your message to help, other people will line up to have time with you. If you stay focused on serving others with your message, the longer you live, the deeper and more powerful it will become. As you integrate every experience—every circle—and grow in maturity, your story will become a great gift to the world. The longer you live, layering one perspective on top of another, the more your life becomes a work of art that speaks to the world.

So, let's talk about how to do that.

Writing the Book on Your Life

I've worked with lots of people who want to share their message but don't know where to start. I usually recommend they start by mapping out their story. The framework I shared in this book is a tool that I've used to help people get perspective on God's work in their life and find their mission and message. Whenever people don't know where to start, I have them take each season and break it down into circles.

Here's the process:

1. Take a look at the circle pattern below. What was the turning point that started the season you're in right now? Write it down next to the turning point.

2. Identify where you think you are right now in the circle.

3. Break down specific events in your current season that roughly match up with each stage of the circle. For the adventure section, write down the top three greatest challenges you faced during that phase of the journey.

4. Then, do the same for the season just prior to this one.

Just the process of doing this can help you start to connect the dots of meaning and purpose. It can help you keep your faith strong and perspective lifted as you begin to see the pattern of God's work emerge in your life.

Each season tends to have a key truth we learned—a message. When you combine all those revelations and new perspectives, it's pretty common to see a theme emerge—a life message.

Once they've broken down their life into those circles, I ask them this: If you were to talk to someone who is struggling with similar issues, what would you tell them are the top five to ten things you've learned about how to face those challenges? What are the messages that emerged in your life from each season?

Write those things down—whether it's two things or twenty things.

Then, take a bunch of blank pages of paper. At the top of each page, write one of those points you made on the list and a brief explanation of why you think that thing is important.

Write down what you've learned about God and yourself through those key points. Write down any truths from the Bible that have inspired or helped you during the journey to learning those key message points.

That's how you shift your story into a message.

And that, my friends, is how you write a book. I also believe it's how you begin to really explore the meaning and purpose that God has been building into your life and the masterpiece He's been creating with it.

Young Geniuses and Old Masters

A guy named David Galenson did some research trying to figure out at what age artists, authors, and creatives produce their greatest work. He concluded that there are two types of creative geniuses: conceptual and experimental.

The conceptual innovator hits peak creativity early in life. They find a new form of art or a new way to create. Artists like Vermeer, van Gogh, Picasso, and Herman Melville created the art and books that made them famous when they were still in their twenties and thirties. They were Young Geniuses.[6]

But the Old Masters, the artists whose works have gained massive acclaim, tend to be experimental innovators—people who spend a lifetime of trial and error, building and learning, until they arrive at what becomes their masterpiece. Michelangelo, Leonardo da Vinci, and Rembrandt were Old Masters. Their works, hanging in museums all around the world, were created later in their lives. The final product didn't happen all at once; it was created slowly. In fact, scans have been done of the works of many of these painters, and they discovered that the final project we all acknowledge as a masterpiece, what we see on the canvas, is the result of layers and layers of previous attempts and adjustments to the picture.

Old Masters do their greatest work later in life largely due to circle after circle of artistic experimentation. Galenson says that many of the greatest artists spent years perfecting their craft and, in the words of Carl Jung, "circumambulating"—going around an idea until they landed on the fullness of that idea. I think this understanding of what makes for great art has huge implications for the work of art that God is making from your life.

If you're reading this book, it's highly probable that you feel like you haven't quite landed on what you were made to do. You know there's more in you. Your masterpiece isn't quite done. I feel that way a lot. I don't know about you, but Galenson's study is encouraging for me.

What if our greatest work is still ahead?

We've been preparing. We've learned through trial and error. We've been layering and tweaking, learning and growing. God has been pulling things out of us we didn't know were there. All that trial and error has humbled us and taught us wisdom. Now it's time to do our greatest work. It's time to share a message with the world that we are uniquely qualified to share.

Life happens in seasons. Each season has growth and setbacks and setups. You can hold onto faith, being confident that God really is working all things together for your good. The seasons that seem like a waste will often end up being the seasons when you were planting seeds that bring a harvest much further down the road.

In Habakkuk, the famous verse about vision says: "The vision awaits its appointed time."[7] King Solomon says, "For everything there is a season, and a time for every matter under heaven."[8] As your circle expands, little by little, you may find yourself stepping into what you dreamed about many circles ago. A new circle of adventure will begin. Your experience in the circles and seasons of life will have prepared and expanded your capacity. You're ready for it now. Now is your time. Get out there and share the message of God's work in your life.

Consider a movie: it consists of thousands upon thousands of individual pictures, and each of them makes sense and carries a meaning, yet the meaning of the whole film cannot be seen before its last sequence is shown. However, we cannot understand the whole film without having first understood each of its components, each of the individual pictures. Isn't it the same with life? Doesn't the final meaning of life, too, reveal itself, if at all, only at its end, on the verge of death? And doesn't this final meaning, too, depend on whether or not the potential meaning of each single situation has been actualized to the best of their respective individual's knowledge and belief?

—*Viktor Frankl*

Small Group Guide

Dear Reader,

My prayer is that this book will help you see God's hand at work in your life, even when you didn't realize He was working. Through my own personal experience and through coaching lots of others, I've seen that sharing your story helps you gain perspective on the circular patterns of what God has been doing in your life.

With that in mind, one of the best ways to get the most from this book is to invite a group of friends to work through the chapters together—telling and listening to each other's stories along the way. I've created this short leader's guide to give you a simple framework for hosting a small group.

Here are a few suggestions for how to use the book and this leader's guide:

- Plan to meet consistently once per week or every other week. There is a group discussion guide for each chapter of the book (ten chapters). Some people choose to cover one chapter per week; others want to do several. Work through the book in whatever timeframe and manner fits your group best.

- Have each team member highlight (or write down) specific lines and parts of the book that they found particularly relevant as they read.
- Plan to go through the material each time you meet, but if you find that someone in the group is struggling with something, forget the material! Minister to the needs of that person. You can always go over the content of the book later. The content is just the excuse to get together. The most important thing is taking time to engage in each other's stories and experiences.

Since people will be telling some of their personal stories, make sure you make it clear to the team that anything discussed in the group should be kept confidential.

I pray this book inspires and encourages you as you walk through the material in community.

Your Circular Story

Text: (Read aloud to the group) Ecclesiastes 3:1–9, Psalm 23

Key Point: Life happens in seasons. Every season has a purpose in God's master plan for you. Psalm 23 says our Shepherd leads us in "paths made of circles [Hebrew: *magol*] of righteousness." God's work in our life tends to look more like an ever-widening spiral than a straight line.

Reflection: Have each group member share what they highlighted or anything that stood out to them in the reading this week.

Questions:

1. When you think about God's work being more of a circle than a straight line, what thoughts come to your mind about your personal story? Are there any recurring themes, time frames, or situations in your life that you can think of?

2. Based on the breakdown of each stage in Chapter 0, what stage of the journey do you think you might be in right now? (You can use the chart on the following page to identify it.)

Application: Have each member share one thing they want to start applying in their life this week based on what was discussed.

The Turning Point

Text: (Read aloud to the group) Ecclesiastes 3:1–9

Key Point: Every new season starts with a turning point that changes your life. A turning point usually comes with lots of uncertainty, shaking, and maybe some chaos. But it's not the end; it's just the beginning of God preparing you for what He has ahead.

Reflection: Have each group member share what they highlighted or anything that stood out to them in the reading this week.

Questions:
1. Read the list of turning points below aloud and ask group members to raise their hand if they have ever experienced that specific one:
- Parents getting a divorce
- Moving to a new city
- A miscarriage
- A life-threatening illness
- Loss of a loved one
- A mystical moment of connection with something "otherworldly"
- Divorce or separation
- Getting married

- Getting pregnant
- The birth of a child
- Adopting a child
- Fostering a child
- Infertility
- Abandonment
- Betrayal
- Job changes (getting hired or fired)
- Reading a book that changed your perspective

Which turning point would you say had the greatest impact or was most difficult for you?

Application: Have each member share one thing they want to start applying in their life this week based on what was discussed.

The Courage

Text: (Read aloud to the group) 1 John 4:17–19

Key Point: In every new season, a level of courage will be required to face the unknown and step out in faith, with no guarantee of a positive outcome.

Reflection: Have each group member share what they highlighted or anything that stood out to them in the reading this week.

Questions:

1. When it comes to stepping out in courage, which of the following is your greatest struggle? (Feel free to add to the list if one of these doesn't describe your struggle.)

   a. Analysis paralysis (overthinking)
   b. Feeling unqualified/disqualified
   c. Fear of looking foolish
   d. Timing: feeling like a few more things need to be in order before you take the risk
   e. Opposition: concerns about what people will think or getting resistance

2. What has been your personal experience with God's perfect love driving out fear in your life?

Application: Have each member share one thing they want to start applying in their life this week based on what was discussed.

WEEK 4

The Guide

Text: (Read aloud to the group) John 16:12–15

Key Point: In every great adventure story, a guide appears to help the adventurer along the way. As Christ-followers, our Guide is the Holy Spirit, Who gives us direction and insight on the journey. There is no formula for life; there is only revelation of truth from the Holy Spirit.

Reflection: Have each group member share what they highlighted or anything that stood out to them in the reading this week.

Questions:

1. How has the Holy Spirit appeared as a Guide in your life during this or a previous season? (Example: A specific scripture, a book you read, a mentor you met, a friend who came into our life at the perfect time.)

2. If you really believed the Holy Spirit was guiding you, even when you didn't realize it, what difference would that make in how you live your life on a daily basis?

Application: Have each member share one thing they want to start applying in their life this week based on what was discussed.

The Decision

Text: (Read aloud to the group) Luke 9:57–62

Key Point: To get the full benefits of a life of faith in each season, at some point, we have to go all in on the journey. We have to surrender the outcome and throw ourselves into the adventure. Halfway commitment won't work—you have to make the decision to fully engage and be present in the season.

Reflection: Have each group member share what they highlighted or anything that stood out to them in the reading this week.

Questions:
1. In your current season, what decisions did you have to make to go all in and totally commit to being present and engaged?
2. Are there any decisions you've been hesitant to make because of what total commitment will require from you?
3. In Luke 9 (this week's passage), Jesus didn't seem to have a lot of patience for people who wouldn't make a total and immediate commitment to follow Him. Why do you think He was so serious about total commitment?

Application: Have each member share one thing they want to start applying in their life this week based on what was discussed.

The Adventure
(aka The Challenges)

Text: (Read aloud to the group) James 1:2–3, Romans 5:3–5

Key Point: Every season comes with struggles and challenges that stretch us and make us grow. If we can see the struggles as an adventure that is preparing us for future glory, it can help us find meaning and learn what we need to learn in the season.

Reflection: Have each group member share what they highlighted or anything that stood out to them in the reading this week.

Questions:
1. What is the greatest struggle you are facing in this current season?
2. How have the challenges of previous seasons prepared you or made you stronger for what you are facing today?

Application: Have each member share one thing they want to start applying in their life this week based on what was discussed.

WEEK 7

The Dark Cave

Text: (Read aloud to the group) John 15:1–7

Key Point: In every season, we enter a period of darkness where we face off with things we'd rather avoid. Often, we feel God is silent just when we need Him most. It's during those times of pruning, when God seems to be taking away what we love most, that—if we respond correctly—we grow our trust in God's ability to carry us through the struggle.

Questions:
1. Have you ever felt like God had forgotten about you or that your prayers weren't being heard? What was the situation?
2. A. W. Tozer said,

> "It is doubtful whether God can bless a man greatly until he has hurt him deeply." God actually raises up storms of conflict in relationships at times in order to accomplish that deeper work in our character. We cannot love our enemies in our own strength. This is graduate-level grace. Are you willing to enter this school? Are you willing to take the test? If you pass, you can expect to be elevated to a new level in the Kingdom. For He brings us

through these tests as preparation for greater use in the Kingdom. You must pass the test first.

What do you think of this statement? Share your thoughts with the group.

Application: Have each member share one thing they want to start applying in their life this week based on what was discussed.

WEEK 8

The Resolution

Text: (Read aloud to the group) Romans 8:27–31, Genesis 32:22–32

Key Point: After the Dark Cave, there comes a time of resolution—a calm after the storm. Sometimes we emerge from the battle with a limp or wounds. In this stage, we have to take time to evaluate the journey and what it has taught us. We have to choose to let go of the hurt, disappointment, and pain from the season and reframe what we experienced in the light of God's hand at work in our lives.

Reflection: Have each group member share what they highlighted or anything that stood out to them in the reading this week.

Questions:

1. When Jacob wrestled with God and asked for a blessing, the encounter left him with a permanent limp as a reminder of that experience. Have you ever felt like a season of life left you with a limp (emotionally, spiritually, physically)? What did that limp feel/look like?

2. Why do you think so many people never take time to slow down and evaluate after a difficult season but instead just rush ahead or act like it never happened?

Application: Have each member share one thing they want to start applying in their life this week based on what was discussed.

The New Perspective

Text: (Read aloud to the group) 2 Corinthians 3:17–18

Key Point: Every season of life has something to teach us. When we learn something new, our perspective changes: our perspective on the world, on God, and on ourselves. We tend to be a little less certain and a little more humble. When we've properly processed what happened, looking back, we can see how God used that season to prepare us. Armed with the perspective, we really can have confidence that God was working all things together for our good.

Reflection: Have each group member share what they highlighted or anything that stood out to them in the reading this week.

Questions:
1. What changes of perspective have you had about God and yourself in the past few years?
2. Can you relate to the feeling that, in some ways, you are "half the person you used to be"?

Application: Have each member share one thing they want to start applying in their life this week based on what was discussed.

The Message

Text: (Read aloud to the group) Philippians 1:12–14, Revelation 12:11

Key Point: In every season of life, God was preparing you with a message to share and a problem to solve. Your story has given you a message—a testimony—to share with the world around you. Sharing that message will bring meaning and purpose in your life.

Reflection: Have each group member share what they highlighted or anything that stood out to them in the reading this week.

Questions:
1. How have your past experiences prepared you for what you are doing in this season?
2. If you met someone who was going through a struggle similar to something you've experienced in one of your seasons, what would you say are the top three most important lessons you learned in that season that could encourage them in their struggle?

Application: Have each member share one thing they want to start applying in their life this week based on what was discussed.

Notes

Chapter 0: Your Circular Story

1. Viktor Frankl, *Man's Search for Meaning* (New York: Simon and Schuster, 1985), 135.
2. Romans 8:18 NIV
3. 2 Corinthians 4:16–17
4. Ephesians 2:10
5. Ecclesiastes 1:9
6. Romans 11:29; see also Psalm 139:13–14
7. C. G. Jung, *Memories, Dreams, Reflections* (New York: Vintage Books, 1989), 196.
8. Philippians 2:12–13 NIV
9. Ephesians 2:10
10. 2 Corinthians 5:14 NIV
11. G. K. Chesterton, *Orthodoxy* (San Francisco, California: Ignatius Press, 1995), 66.

Chapter 1: The Turning Point

1. Romans 11:29
2. 1 John 3:2
3. Jordan Peterson, *12 Rules for Life* (Toronto: Random House Canada, 2018), 223.
4. 2 Corinthians 5:13–14 NIV; see also Romans 5:3–4
5. G. K. Chesterton, *On Running after One's Hat and Other Whimsies* (New York: Robert M. McBride & Company, 1933), 6.

Chapter 2: The Courage

1. Luke 9:24 NIV
2. See Diane Osborn, ed., *Reflections on the Art of Living: A Joseph Campbell Companion* (New York: Harper Perennial, 1995), 24. This saying is attributed to Joseph Campbell, and a variation of it can be found in this source.

3. G. K. Chesterton, *What's Wrong with the World* (Mineola, New York: Dover Publications, 2007), 192.
4. Matthew 6:33
5. 1 John 4:18 NIV
6. See Romans 5:5
7. See 2 Corinthians 5:14
8. Romans 8:39
9. Proverbs 9:10
10. See Matthew 16:27
11. See Matthew 25:14–30
12. Theodore Roosevelt, "Citizenship in a Republic," speech, The Sorbonne, April 23, 1910, Paris, France, https://www.presidency.ucsb.edu/documents/address-the-sorbonne-paris-france-citizenship-republic.
13. See Ephesians 2:8–10
14. Roy Williams, *Magical Worlds of the Wizard of Ads* (Austin, Texas: Bard Press, 2001), 68.
15. Romans 8:31

Chapter 3: The Guide
1. Carl Jung, *Collected Works 11: Psychology and Religion: West and East* (Princeton, New Jersey: Princeton University Press, 1969).
2. John 16:12–13
3. Matthew 5:20 NIV
4. For more about Mike and to join him on one of his adventures, check out https://www.cleanwaterclimb.net.
5. Isaiah 30:21
6. See "Homily VII on 1 John 4:4–12," Christian Classics Ethereal Library, https://www.ccel.org/ccel/schaff/npnf107.iv.x.html. The full quote is "Once for all, then, a short precept is given thee: Love, and do what thou wilt: whether thou hold thy peace, through love hold thy peace; whether thou cry out, through love cry out; whether thou correct, through love correct; whether thou spare, through love do thou spare: let the root of love be within, of this root can nothing spring but what is good."
7. See 1 Corinthians 13:12
8. Proverbs 27:6 NIV
9. James 1:5
10. Romans 8:11
11. 1 Kings 19:12 NIV

Chapter 4: The Decision
1. Luke 22:42
2. C. S. Lewis to Father Peter Bide, April 29, 1959, in *The Collected Letters of C.S. Lewis*, ed. Walter Hooper, vol. 3, *1950–1963* (New York: HarperOne, 2007).
3. Ecclesiastes 7:10
4. Matthew 6:34 NIV
5. Luke 9:60–62 NIV
6. G. K. Chesterton, *What's Wrong with the World* (Mineola, New York: Dover Publications, 2007), 29.
7. Psalm 103:2
8. Ephesians 3:20 KJV
9. Basil King, *The Conquest of Fear* (Good Press, 1921), Kindle Edition.
10. See Philippians 4:7 NIV

Chapter 5: The Adventure (aka The Challenges)
1. See Nassim Nicholas Taleb, *Antifragile: Things that Gain from Disorder* (New York: Random House Trade Paperbacks, 2014).
2. Acts 14:22 NIV
3. Proverbs 28:1
4. 2 Corinthians 12:9
5. James 1:2–4
6. Matthew 5:44
7. Genesis 50:20–21 NIV
8. Quoted in Robert McKee, *Story: Style, Structure, Substance, and the Principles of Screenwriting* (New York: Regan Books, 1997), 133.
9. Matthew 6:34 NIV
10. Hebrews 12:7 NIV
11. 2 Corinthians 12:9 NIV
12. 2 Corinthians 4:17

Chapter 6: The Dark Cave
1. John 6:68
2. Saint Teresa of Avila, *The Interior Castle* (Digireads.com Publishing, 2013), Kindle edition.
3. Proverbs 24:10
4. A. W. Tozer, *The Root of the Righteous* (Camp Hill, Pennsylvania: Wingspread Publishers, 2007).
5. John 15:2

6. Michael Meade, *Awakening the Soul: A Deep Response to a Troubled World* (Vashon, Washington: Greenfire Press, 2018).
7. Job 42:3–5 ESV
8. G. K. Chesterton, *The Everlasting Man* (Mansfield Centre, Connecticut: Martino Publishing, 2014), 6.
9. 2 Corinthians 2:14
10. See 2 Corinthians 3:18
11. Henri Nouwen, *The Wounded Healer: Ministry in Contemporary Society* (New York: Image Books, 1979), 72.

Chapter 7: The Resolution

1. *Merriam-Webster*, s.v. "dénouement," https://www.merriam-webster.com/dictionary/denouement.
2. A. W. Tozer, *The Root of the Righteous* (Camp Hill, Pennsylvania: Wingspread Publishers, 2007).
3. 2 Corinthians 12:10
4. Robert Bly, *Iron John: A Book about Men* (Boston, Massachusetts: Da Capo Press, 2015).
5. Rainer Maria Rilke, *Letters to a Young Poet* (New York: W. W. Norton & Company, 1993), 27.

Chapter 8: The New Perspective

1. Ecclesiastes 7:8 NIV
2. "Essential Chesterton," The Society of G. K. Chesterton, https://www.chesterton.org/quotations/essential-chesterton/.
3. 1 Corinthians 4:5
4. 2 Corinthians 4:18
5. Colossians 1:16–17
6. Ephesians 4:15–16
7. M. Scott Peck, *The Road Less Traveled: A New Psychology of Love, Traditional Values, and Spiritual Growth* (New York: Touchstone, 2003), 81.
8. 1 Corinthians 13:4–7
9. 1 Corinthians 8:1–2 NIV
10. Philippians 2:6–7 NIV
11. See Matthew 5:5
12. Janet O. Hagberg and Robert A. Guelich, *The Critical Journey: Stages in the Life of Faith* (Salem, Wisconsin: Sheffield Publishing Company, 1995), 33.
13. Galatians 5:6 NIV
14. James 3:13 NKJV

Chapter 9: The Message

1. Richard Rohr, *Falling Upward: A Spirituality for the Two Halves of Life* (San Francisco: Jossey-Bass, 2011), 34.
2. Matthew 5:14–16
3. Revelation 12:11 NIV
4. Colossians 1:24
5. John Piper, "Filling Up What Is Lacking in Christ's Afflictions," Desiring God, October 19, 2008, https://www.desiringgod.org/messages/filling-up-what-is-lacking-in-christs-afflictions.
6. See David Galenson, *Old Masters and Young Geniuses: The Two Life Cycles of Artistic Creativity* (Princeton: Princeton University Press, 2006).
7. Habakkuk 2:3
8. Ecclesiastes 3:1